FLORENTINE

Emiko Davies

FLORENTINE

THE TRUE CUISINE
OF FLORENCE

hardie grant books

Introduction

In Florence, history has a way of weaving itself through every aspect of life, and food is no exception. The kitchen staples and many of the favourite dishes of the Renaissance city's cuisine are much the same as they were during Dante's medieval Florence or Catherine de' Medici's sixteenth century because, as locals like to say, '*squadra che vince non si cambia*' – in other words, you should not (and need not) change a good thing.

A stroll through the city's streets – past pastry shops bustling with espresso-sippers, busy lunchtime trattorias, food vans selling tripe sandwiches and charming hole-in-the-wall wine bars – reveals how Florentines remain proudly attached to their unchanging cuisine, a cuisine that tells the unique story of its city, dish by dish.

The Florentines, like most Italians, have a very important relationship with their food. There are rules about what can be eaten when, with what accompaniments and in what particular order. Seasons and traditions play an important role in the kitchen and you can easily tell the time of year by simply looking at a Florentine menu, bakery window or market stall.

Florentine cuisine is earthy and rustic, at times even austere. In his 2003 book *Cucina Fiorentina*, Tuscan gastronome and journalist Aldo Santini compares it to 'a man with his head screwed on'. Not extravagant, but reliable and modest. Sincere and straightforward. Although simple, it is prepared with pride and care, and makes particularly good use of bread and olive oil, two of the cuisine's staple ingredients.

In his introduction to *The Decameron*, fourteenth-century Florentine author Giovanni Boccaccio (1313–1375) recounts how some Florentines attempted to 'live better' and avoid the plague by following a philosophy of '*Delicatissimi cibi e ottimi vini temperatissimamente usando, e ogni lussuria fuggendo...*' In other words, delicate food and very good wines, used with care and avoiding every luxury. In many ways, this is still the Florentine approach to food.

With a nod to medieval origins, many dishes reflect the ethos of not letting anything go to waste. The Florentines are masters of thrift, using up what others would normally throw out. They make the most of stale bread, chicken livers, *lampredotto* (abomasum tripe) and even roosters' combs – although this once popular Renaissance dish, known as *cibreo*, is almost extinct today. All of these ingredients are carefully prepared in characteristically simple ways, unique to Florence, in dishes such as *ribollita*, *crostini di fegatini* and *lampredotto panini*. Not only are these ingredients a model of economy in the kitchen, but they are also exalted, with these well-known dishes being elevated to hero status in the city.

Florentine food journalist Leonardo Romanelli points out that the only weakness in the local cuisine is dessert. Missing a sweet tooth, many of Florence's traditional sweets are either bread-based, such as the autumnal *schiacciata all'uva* (grape focaccia), *pandiramerino* (raisin and rosemary buns) and *schiacciata alla fiorentina* (a yeasted cake dusted with powdered sugar); or they are deep-fried and are strictly a winter Carnival treat, such as *cenci* and *frittelle* (rice fritters). Zuccotto is the closest thing to a proper dessert, resembling a bright pink version of the dome of Florence's Duomo, with Alchermes-dipped sponge encasing a rich ricotta and chocolate filling. It seems like a relative of trifle or even tiramisu, and is sometimes served frozen like semifreddo. And then there are, of course, *cantuccini* (almond biscotti), the preferred way to end a meal at a Florentine table, with a glass of sweet vin santo for dipping and inspiring conversation.

It goes without saying that Florence is a city that lives in its past. Its medieval and Renaissance history, immortalised in famous buildings, sculptures and paintings, is the main reason the city is as loved and visited as it is today. In every nook and cranny, history seeps out onto the well-trodden stone streets and into the every day.

Food in the Renaissance

The Renaissance was a period of enormous change, not only in the world of art and architecture, or even politics, but also in gastronomy. The same sensibility that was being used in art was influencing dishes in Florentine kitchens, and the subsequent banquets in noble palazzi.

During this time, cooking techniques improved and became more sophisticated, while aesthetics and presentation of food became more important than ever. Cheese-making techniques were much the same as they are today. Apparently Michelangelo would request seasonal pecorino cheese (known as marzolino cheese) be sent to him from Florence when he was working in Rome. The discovery of the New World in 1492 also brought a plethora of new and exotic ingredients to experiment with in the kitchen. These ingredients gave rise to more refined and elegant food.

At the 1469 wedding of Lorenzo the Magnificent (1449–1492) – Florence's beloved ruler and benefactor to artists such as Michelangelo and Botticelli – there was a deliberately modest public feast, where 400 of the town's citizens were invited to share in the event. The simple menu consisted of savoury appetisers, boiled and roasted meat, biscuits and candied fruits.

Three years earlier, for the marriage of Lorenzo's sister, Nannina, into Florence's powerful Ruccellai family, celebrations were more extravagant, yet still refined. Fifty cooks fed over 500 people over three days.

Boiled tongue and *biancomangiare* were served at the first course: a delicate dish and enormously popular in the Renaissance, *biancomangiare* was made with finely pounded, poached chicken breast cooked with almond milk, white bread and sugar until creamy, then garnished with rosewater or spices. It had a beautifully creamy texture and a delicate but perfectly balanced flavour, and was made using techniques that ensured that it remained perfectly white in colour. It is a wonderful example of how the culinary arts went through a Renaissance as much as the rest of the arts, taking a giant leap from the rough gruels of the Middle Ages.

This course was followed by roast meats garnished with rosewater, then cold meats and jellied fish, and then a second roast. The food, as characterised by this period and by its leaders, was splendid and refined, but not at all over the top.

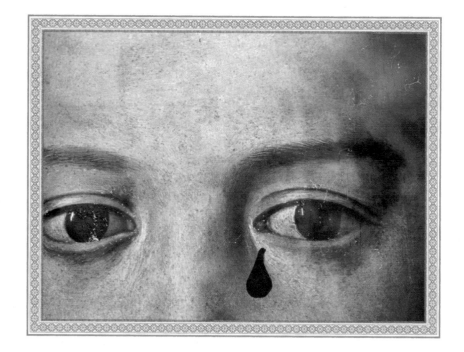

AN ARTIST'S FOOD DIARY

Pontormo (1494–1557), an often misunderstood Mannerist artist, kept a diary between 1554 and 1556, the years just before his death. It was very much a food journal and, in between little sketches, a humble account of a modest Renaissance diet.

He mentions some of the fantastic meals he enjoyed with his star pupil and good friend, Bronzino. In one entry, he writes that after one such long Sunday lunch, which turned into supper, he fasted until Wednesday when he could finally bring himself to have 'some Trebbiano and a couple of eggs'. He goes on to list, almost daily, his main meals: a cabbage and an omelette; half of the head of a kid and soup; zibibbo grapes, bread and capers in salad; mutton soup; an omelette with broad beans and some caviar; some dried figs. He even mentions eating rosemary bread, still a favourite bakery find known as *pandiramerino*.

THE RENAISSANCE SUPPER CLUB

While Pontormo's notes on his everyday diet is a modest and revealing account of the solitary life of an old but determined artist, a little earlier in 1512, twelve of Florence's most famous artists and poets had formed a sort of Renaissance supper club.

As Renaissance artist and biographer, Giorgio Vasari (1511–1574) narrates, La Compagnia del Paiolo consisted of a group of artists who were to contribute creative, aesthetically pleasing dinners for each other, one more inventive than the next. Each member could bring along four friends for dinner (Michelangelo, Botticelli and even Leonardo da Vinci are said to have participated), with the main objective being simple merry-making.

The architect and sculptor Giovanni Francesco Rustici (1475–1554) once invited his guests to eat in what seemed to be a giant, steaming *trompe l'oeil tub* (a reference to the *paiolo* of the club's name, a large copper pot for cooking over a fire). Guests sat around the edge of the pot and dishes were held up on the boughs of a moving tree. Meanwhile, the painter Andrea del Sarto (1486–1530) once contributed a gastronomic version of Florence's Baptistery, complete with columns made of sausages and a marble floor of *soprassata* (a favourite Tuscan salume similar to brawn or head-cheese), decorated with a choir book made of sheets of lasagne and a choir of roasted birds.

The Nineteenth Century to Today

The nineteenth-century gastronome, Pellegrino Artusi (1820–1911), is considered the great-grandfather of Italian cooking. His self-published cookbook of 790 recipes, *Science in the Kitchen and the Art of Eating Well*, was written from his Florentine home in Piazza d'Azeglio and published in 1891. This was a first – a cookbook that defined Italian cuisine as a national cuisine. Just three decades earlier, the regional peninsula had been unified into one Italy, and for a brief period between 1865 and 1871, Florence was named its capital.

Artusi was a native of Emilia-Romagna who spent a significant part of his life in Florence. His cookbook is peppered with very good Florentine and other Tuscan dishes, many of which are still cooked the way he describes. His book became a national bestseller and is still present in the majority of Italian kitchens today.

Piero Camporesi, the editor of the 1970 edition of *Science in the Kitchen*, goes as far as to suggest that it was Artusi's cookbook that helped bring the country and its diverse dialects together into one national language. In the *Oxford Companion to Italian Food*, Gillian Riley paints this picture: 'While the *questione della lingua* [question of language] was being debated by academics, innocent housewives throughout the land were consulting their 'Artusi' every day, and his literate, slightly colloquial, Florentine version of Tuscan … became reassuringly familiar.'

In 1927, Giulio Gandi wrote *Antiche e caratteristiche trattorie fiorentine* (Antique and characteristic Florentine trattorie), which gives interesting insights into which dishes were on the tables nearly a century ago. He describes Florence's best specialities as 'the famous *bistecca*' (Florentine steak) and stewed white beans dressed simply in olive oil from the Florentine hills. He also mentions deep-fried chicken and artichokes, *arista* (Florentine roast pork), *fegatelli* (pork liver parcels), *ribollita* and deep-fried fish pulled right out of the Arno river. All, except for the fish, are still on the menus of Florence's best and most traditional trattorie.

No longer is Florence considered a city of innovation, inspiration and modernity, and neither is it a city that is ruled by its gastronomy, which is made of dishes that are the direct descendants of those written about by Dante, Boccaccio and Bronzino. Its unique and unpretentious cuisine remains little known in the gastronomic world – under the shadow of the Tuscan region as a whole, perhaps. But in the same way that history weaves its way into anything you explore in depth in Florence, so is the cuisine formed by its fantastic history, helped by its fortunate position in the centre of Tuscany, where good olive oil, good wine and abundant produce have always been readily available. Fortunately for all good food lovers, its proud, headstrong people have shown as much dedication to preserving the city's favourite dishes as they have the famous buildings and art.

Notes About the Recipes

Recipes were tested on a standard gas cooktop. You may need to adjust cooking times slightly for induction or electric cooktops.

Baking recipes were all tested in a conventional oven with an oven thermometer. If using a fan-forced oven, you may need to adjust the temperature or cooking times slightly.

Eggs used were medium-sized, free-range eggs (55 g/1¾ oz).

When a recipe calls for olive oil, always use extra-virgin olive oil except in the case of deep-frying, where a regular not-too-fruity olive oil with a lighter flavour, should be used.

Some Tips

BAKING BREAD

Use a setting that distributes heat equally from the top and bottom of the oven (most importantly the bottom). You may need to place the bread on a low shelf to make sure that it cooks well from underneath.

BLIND BAKING

Blind baking helps to ensure that the bottom crust of a tart cooks through properly. Place a sheet of baking paper over the pastry and fill with baking beads (you can also use dried beans or uncooked rice – discard afterwards or you can keep these 'baking beans' in a jar and re-use specifically for this purpose). Bake in the oven as per the recipe, then remove the paper and beads and continue with the recipe.

CROSTINI AND CROSTONI

It is ideal to use lightly toasted, stale bread for these, as they do in Florence. An oven or grill (broiler) is preferable to a toaster. If using fresh bread, simply dry out the bread by baking in a very low oven until the bread slices are just dry to the touch, not coloured or turned into crisps.

GELATO-MAKING

The recipes here work best with an ice cream machine. Homemade gelato usually benefits from a rest in the freezer for about an hour before serving. If it has been in the freezer for overnight or longer, remove the gelato about 15 minutes before serving.

YEAST AND RISING DOUGH

In Italy, fresh yeast is readily available at supermarkets and is frequently used. Dried yeast commonly comes in two forms: active dry yeast and instant (rapid-rise) yeast. They can be used interchangeably but the recipes here use active dry yeast, which needs to be dissolved first in warm water. Instant yeast can be mixed directly into the dough and does not need proving time.

If you want to double any of the yeasted bread recipes, don't double the yeast but give it a longer rise. There'll be enough there to work on double the rest of the ingredients. As a very simple rule, the less yeast used, the longer it will need to rise (overnight in the refrigerator is best) and with a longer rise you will be rewarded with a better developed flavour, a better texture and longer lasting bread. But if you're in a hurry and you only have time to let the bread rise for 1 hour (as a minimum), keep it in a warm place to encourage it to rise more quickly. If it is winter and your kitchen is cold, you can even warm up the oven a little, turn it off, then place the bowl in the warmed oven.

If using active dry yeast and you're not sure how old it is, do a quick test to check it's still alive and well. Place the required amount of yeast in 125 ml (4 fl oz/½ cup) warm water and a pinch of sugar. Stir to dissolve then let sit 10 minutes. If the yeast is still active, there will be foam and bubbles – and quite a bit of them. If this doesn't happen, discard the yeast and buy some new yeast. If all is good you can use this mixture in the recipe, taking into consideration the water measurement.

LA PASTICCERIA

The Pastry Shop

Crostata *di* Marmellata
APRICOT JAM CROSTATA

Crema Pasticcera
PASTRY CREAM

Cornetti
ITALIAN BRIOCHE CROISSANTS

Sfogliatine
SWEET PUFF PASTRIES

Budini *di* Riso
RICE PUDDINGS

Bomboloncini
DOUGHNUT HOLES

Frittelle *di* Riso
RICE FRITTERS

Torta *di* Mele
APPLE CAKE

Torta *di* Semolino e Cioccolato
SEMOLINA & CHOCOLATE TART

Torta *di* Pera e Cioccolato
PEAR & CHOCOLATE CAKE

Torta *della* Nonna
GRANDMOTHER'S TART

Fritelle *di* Riso
RICE FRITTERS

Zuccotto
RICOTTA AND CHOCOLATE FILLED SPONGE CAKE

'Breakfast usually consists of a pastry – consumed while standing at the counter, artfully avoiding powdery icing sugar falling over clothes – followed by an espresso coffee, pulled hard and fast, and finished even faster.'

The Florentine breakfast is a reliably quick affair. It can be eaten while on the go and paid for in pocket change. It usually consists of a pastry – consumed while standing at the counter, artfully avoiding powdery icing sugar falling over clothes – followed by an espresso coffee, pulled hard and fast, and finished even faster. This morning ritual is just as often done in the neighbourhood *pasticceria* (pastry shop) as it is at the *bar* (a coffee shop), and it is an integral part of the Florentine lifestyle.

Whether short, long, 'stained' (*macchiato*) or cappuccino, coffee usually accompanies an enticing pastry, chosen from a smooth glass counter. Sweet brioche-like croissants known as cornetti are found in all forms, from wholemeal with honey to jam-filled or plain except for a lick of sugar syrup over the top. Deep-fried *bomboloni*, plump with jam or *crema* (pastry cream), sit next to *sfoglia* (puff pastry) with caramelised bottoms and crema or rice-filled insides, while hefty slices of blackberry or apricot jam crostata accompany little tarts filled with sweet rice pudding, as well as an array of cakes and seasonal specialities.

The *pasticceria* is also the place to buy a whole cake, like a semolina and ganache tart; or a scarlet-tinged zuccotto, proudly displayed in well-lit fridges; or dainty miniature pastries such as *bigne*; or little cream tarts topped with fresh raspberries to take home. It all gets wrapped up in the pastry shop's own logo-printed paper and tied with a gold ribbon – the perfect little package to take to friends when invited to someone's house or when hosting yourself.

Crostata *di* Marmellata

APRICOT JAM CROSTATA

JAM

500 g (1 lb 2 oz) ripe apricots
200 g (7 oz) sugar

SWEET SHORTCRUST PASTRY

125 g (4½ oz) cold unsalted butter
250 g (9 oz) plain (all-purpose) flour
80 g (2¾ oz) sugar
1 egg, plus 1 egg yolk, beaten
zest of 1 lemon

NOTE

The best test for the jam set is the frozen saucer test. Place a saucer in the freezer and when you want to test how set your jam is, place a teaspoon-sized blob of hot jam onto the cold saucer. Turn it sideways to see how it dribbles and wobbles. For me, this jam is ready when it slides slowly but decisively and wrinkles when poked.

This is a classic recipe for the simplest jam tart pastry with an almost cake-like crumb. Both this jam recipe and pastry recipe are adapted from Pellegrino Artusi's 1891 cookbook, *Science in the Kitchen and the Art of Eating Well.*

Crostata di marmellata is usually made with either blackberry or apricot jam. This silky smooth apricot jam is Artusi's own favourite out of all fruit jams and is ideal for piping into homemade cornetti (page 28) or *bomboloncini* (page 42), or for gliding onto a sweet shortcrust pastry base for a *crostata di marmellata*. You could also substitute peaches for apricots, especially those blushing-rose peaches with yellow flesh. Otherwise, this crostata can be made in a pinch with 250 g (9 oz) of your favourite ready-made jam and by simply following the recipe for the pastry crust.

JAM

Halve the apricots and remove the pits. Put them in a heavy-bottomed saucepan over a low heat, stirring occasionally so the fruit doesn't stick to the bottom of the pan. As the pan heats, the apricots will release their own juices and the fruit will begin to simmer. Let the apricots simmer for approximately 30 minutes, stirring occasionally, or until the fruit is completely soft. Pass the mixture through a food mill or a very fine sieve over a bowl to remove the skins for a smooth fruit purée.

Place the purée back in the saucepan over a low heat and add the sugar. Heat and stir until the sugar dissolves. Turn the heat up to medium and let bubble until the jam reaches the consistency desired. If you let this go quite a while, you will get a harder set jam, but even just a short 10 minutes will give you a nice soft set jam, which is just right for this crostata.

PASTRY AND ASSEMBLY

Chop the cold butter into small pieces. If using a food processor, pulse the flour, sugar and butter until you have a crumbly, sandy texture and there are no more visible pieces of butter. If mixing by hand, rub the butter into the flour and sugar until you achieve the desired result. Mix in the beaten egg and yolk along with the lemon zest, until the pastry comes together into a smooth, elastic ball. Wrap tightly in plastic wrap and rest in the fridge for at least 30 minutes.

Preheat the oven to 180°C (360°F). Grease a 23 cm (9 in) pie dish.

Divide the dough into two pieces, one slightly larger than the other. Roll this larger piece out to about 3 mm (⅛ in) and press into the pie dish. Roll out the rest of the pastry and with a pastry cutter or sharp knife, cut long strips about 2 cm (¾ in) wide. Fill the pie base with jam and criss-cross lattice strips over the top. If you like, use the leftover egg white to brush over the top of the pastry for some shine.

Bake in the oven for about 25 minutes or until golden brown.

MAKES 1 CROSTATA, SERVES 8

Crema Pasticcera
PASTRY CREAM

4 egg yolks
120 g (4½ oz) sugar
30 g (1 oz) cornflour (cornstarch)
500 ml (17 fl oz/2 cups) warm milk
Optional: zest of 1 lemon *or*
    1 teaspoon natural vanilla extract
    or ½ vanilla pod, split open and
    seeds scraped

This is a simple, traditional preparation for pastry cream, a thick Italian custard, which is used to fill pastries such as *bomboloncini* (page 42), cornetti (page 28) and *sfogliatine* (page 34) and to fill cakes such as *schiacciata alla fiorentina* (page 82) or the *torta della nonna* (page 53). Depending on what you are using this pastry cream for, you may like to add some subtle flavour with lemon zest or vanilla. This recipe can easily be halved if you don't need the amount that it makes here.

Whisk the egg yolks and sugar together in a mixing bowl until pale. Stir in the cornflour. Put the mixture in a saucepan over a low heat and add the warm milk, little by little, stirring between each addition. Add the lemon zest or vanilla essence or seeds, if using. Stir continuously with a whisk or a wooden spoon until the mixture becomes smooth and thick, about 10 minutes. You are looking for a consistency similar to mayonnaise (when cool it will also firm up further). Do not let it boil – remove from the heat at the very first sign of a bubble.

Remove the pastry cream from the heat. Prepare an ice bath and cool the pastry cream quickly by transferring to a mixing bowl set over the ice water. Cover with plastic wrap making sure that the plastic is touching the surface of the pastry cream, so it doesn't develop a skin. Keep in the refrigerator until needed.

MAKES ABOUT 680 G (1½ LB) PASTRY CREAM

Cornetti
ITALIAN BRIOCHE CROISSANTS

CORNETTI DOUGH

20 g (¾ oz) fresh yeast, or 7 g
(¼ oz/2½ teaspoons) active
dry yeast

150 ml (5 fl oz) lukewarm water

75 g (2¾ oz) unsalted butter,
softened at room temperature

50 g (1¾ oz) sugar

2 eggs

500 g (1 lb 2 oz/4 cups) bread flour
(see note)

zest of 1 lemon and 1 orange

1 level teaspoon salt

250 g (9 oz) well-chilled unsalted
butter (for the 'butter block';
see note on butter on the
following page)

1 egg, beaten for egg wash

raw (turbinado) sugar for sprinkling,
optional

SUGAR SYRUP

45 g (1½ oz/3 tablespoons) sugar

3 tablespoons water

NOTE

It's best to use a flour that will give
the dough some strength (something
with a protein content of around
12%) for successful stretching and
shaping of the cornetti, so bread flour
is ideal. In Italy it's common to use a
combination of half Manitoba (strong)
flour, which can have a protein
content of 15–18%, and half '00' flour.
If using only a weaker flour, such as
plain (all-purpose) flour, you will risk
the dough ripping when it comes to
shaping or even rising. If you're not
sure how strong your flour is, check
on the nutrition label on the back
of the packet and you should find the
protein content.

Think of cornetti as Italian croissants but with a difference. They're less buttery (and therefore somewhat less flaky), more brioche-like (thanks to the addition of eggs) and, most importantly, they are always sweet, with a distinct citrus perfume. They're a staple of the Florentine *bar* counter or pastry shop and probably the most popular breakfast choice. You can find cornetti of all types: plain, wholewheat, dusted with icing sugar, shiny with sugar syrup, marbled with chocolate, or with a variety of fillings from jam to pastry cream to honey. Many *pasticcerie* will also offer a selection of mignon pastries – that is, dainty half-sized ones, if you only want a small bite to eat.

This recipe, which is inspired partly by Paoletta Sersante's popular blog, *Anice & Cannella*, partly by Carol Field's method in *The Italian Baker* and partly by my own preferences, will give you small, *mignon cornetti vuoti* (or 'empty' cornetti) with a bit of shine from a lick of sugar syrup and some crunch from raw sugar. Once you've perfected these, you may like to try filling them by placing a teaspoon of your favourite jam or other filling such as pastry cream on the widest part of the dough before rolling them up.

While it looks like a lot of work, making cornetti is easier than it seems, mostly involving resting time to make this elastic dough easier to work with, with just a bit of rolling and folding in between. One piece of advice: it is best to work in a cool environment so that the butter doesn't get too soft, so resist the urge to make cornetti on a hot day. An ingenious tip I got from a pastry chef: if you have a warm kitchen, cover the work surface where you will be rolling your cornetti dough with a baking sheet topped with ice or bags of frozen peas, and leave for a while to chill.

I like to make these over two or three days – it seems like a long time but it is very low maintenance this way and will easily fit around a work schedule. By the morning of the last day, which simply consists of shaping the cornetti and letting them rise before baking, you'll be rewarded with some of the best pastries you'll ever taste.

Recipe continued overleaf >

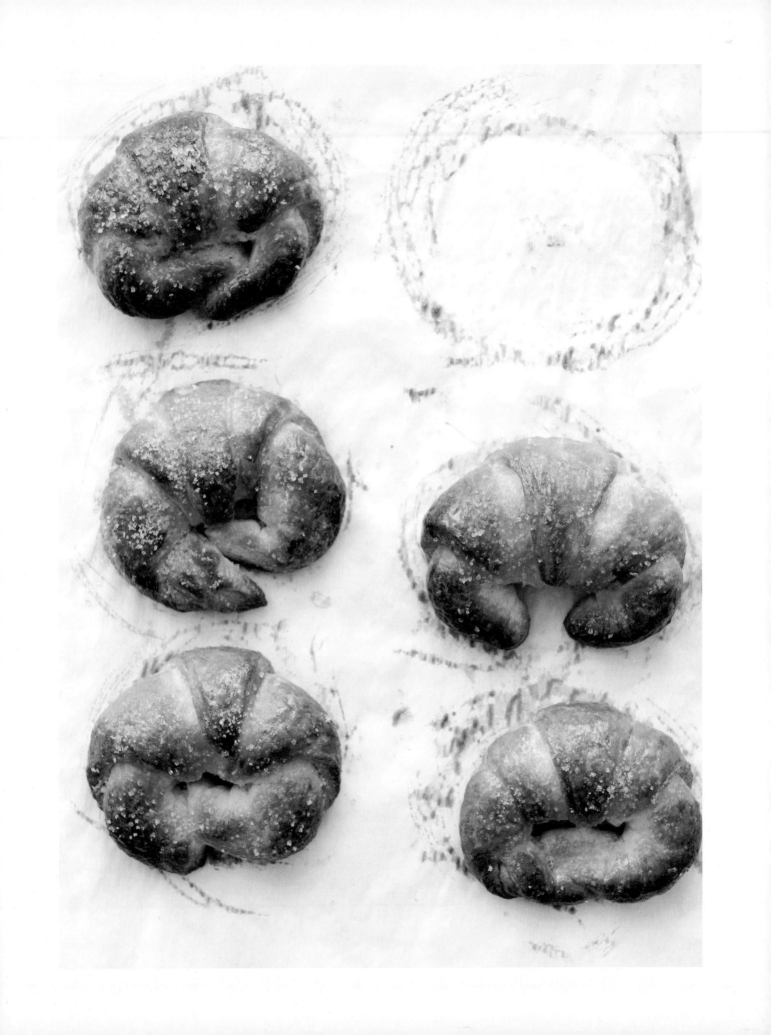

In Italy, butter is unsalted and is very pale, sweet and creamy. If you can, try to use a cultured butter (also known as European-style butter). The difference is that it has a slightly higher fat content, which means it is more pliable (it won't crack when rolled, which can ruin all your hard work), and will create good, flaky layers. Cultured butter also has a more complex flavour – all things which lead to better cornetti.

PREPARE THE DOUGH

Stir the yeast into the lukewarm water in a large bowl until dissolved. In a separate bowl, beat the soft butter into the sugar, add the eggs, then pour this into the yeast mixture and combine.

In a separate bowl, combine the flour, zest and salt. Stir the dry mixture bit by bit into the wet ingredients until the dough comes together (towards the end you may have to use your hands if not using a mixer).

Knead lightly on a floured work surface for 1 minute, or until the dough is smooth. Be careful not to over-knead or you will introduce too much elasticity. Put the dough into a bowl, cover with plastic wrap and let rise for 1–1½ hours or until doubled in size. Remove the dough from the bowl and knead a few times on a lightly floured surface to expel the air, then flatten into a disc. Double wrap the dough tightly in plastic and refrigerate for 4–6 hours or overnight.

THE BUTTER BLOCK

Remove the well-chilled butter from the fridge 30 minutes before you need to use it. Place the butter between two sheets of baking paper and bash with a rolling pin until malleable, but still cold, then shape it into a square, roughly 12.5 cm (5 in) wide.

Roll out the dough to a rough square approximately 23 cm (9 in) wide and 1.5 cm (½ in) thick and place the butter in the centre of the dough at 45 degrees to its edges, so that the corners of the dough can fold perfectly over the edges of the butter block to enclose it like an envelope. Pinch and seal the dough well so that no butter escapes during rolling.

On a lightly floured work surface, roll this dough package forwards and backwards to create a long rectangle about 8 mm (¼ in) thick – the shortest side will be closest to you.

THE TURNS

(See 'The turns' overleaf.) The next series of steps are known as 'turns' and consist of folding the rolled out dough into thirds, turning the dough and rolling and folding again. If at any time it begins to get too difficult to roll the dough or the butter seems too soft, place the dough in the fridge and let rest for a short time, then try again.

For the first set of turns, fold the rectangle into thirds like a business letter: with the shortest side still closest to you, fold the top third down and the bottom third up. Turn the dough 90 degrees to the right (it should look like a book with the 'spine' to the left) and repeat: roll out the dough to a long rectangle 8 mm (¼ in) thick, then fold into thirds. Wrap the dough well in plastic wrap and chill for at least 30 minutes and up to 1 hour.

For the second and third pair of turns, repeat exactly as for the first set but after the third pair of turns, double-wrap the dough (so it does not explode out of the wrap as it gets the urge to rise!) and rest in the refrigerator for 4 hours or overnight, weighed down with a board or a plate and a few cans of beans or similar on top.

Recipe continued overleaf >

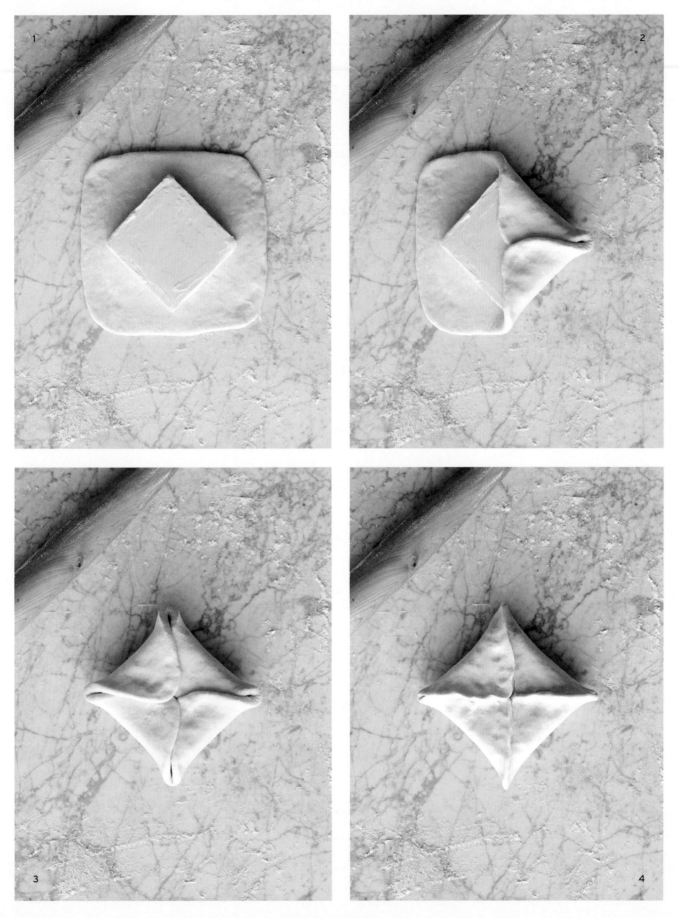

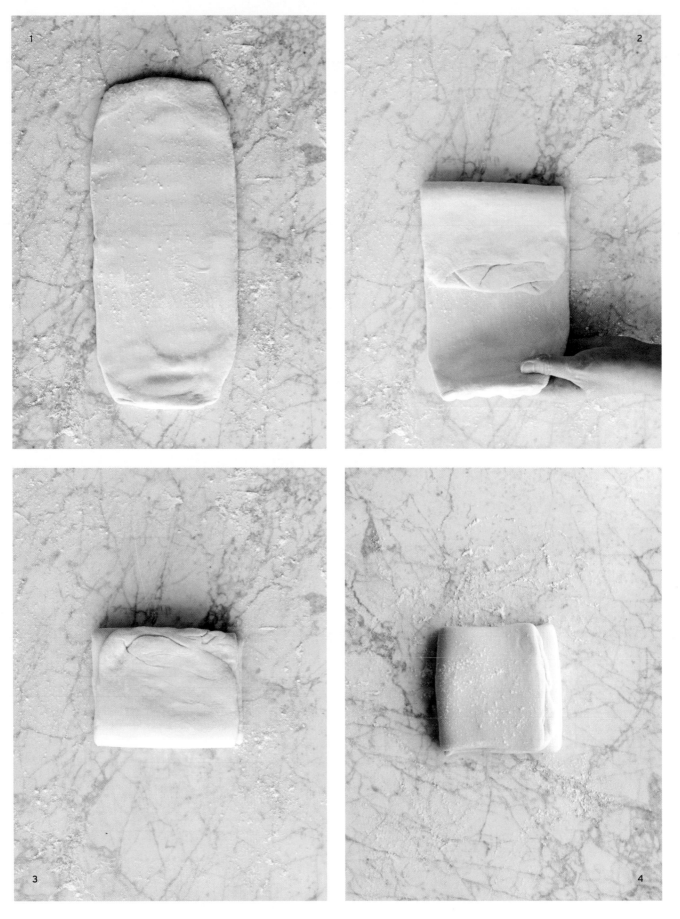

If you want to freeze any of the cornetti, do so directly after shaping. Freeze them on the baking tray, covered in plastic wrap – when they're solid you can transfer them to freezer bags. To bake, place the frozen cornetti on a lined baking tray and thaw in the fridge overnight. The next day, let them rise in a warm place for 2 hours, or until doubled. Bake as described in the recipe.

SHAPING THE CORNETTI

Cut the dough into two even pieces. Keep one piece under a dish towel, chilling in the fridge. On a floured work surface, roll out the other piece of dough into a rectangle about 20 cm (8 in) wide on one side and no more than 8 mm (¼ in) thick. With a very sharp knife or a pizza cutter, cut into two long strips, 10 cm (4 in) tall, and cut each strip into even triangles with a base width of about 12 cm (4½ in). Trim any uneven edges with a knife. Dust lightly with flour if the dough begins to stick. Repeat with the rest of the dough and place unused pieces under a dish towel or loosely cover with plastic wrap to stop the dough from drying out while you shape the cornetti.

Position a triangle with the base towards you and very gently flatten and stretch the dough. To avoid ripping, pull from the centre outwards, not from the tips. Pull the top of the triangle up and stretch the base out wide towards the sides – you should be able to stretch the triangle to about double the height and to at least 17 cm (7 in) wide.

Once stretched, hold the tip of the triangle with one hand, and with the other, roll up from the base to the top, keeping the tip stretched as you go. Tuck the tip underneath the cornetto, facing you. On a baking tray lined with baking paper, place the cornetti about 5 cm (2 in) apart to make room for rising (it is very difficult to move them after they have risen) and pull the ends into a crescent shape, bringing them together in front. Repeat with the rest of the dough.

Loosely cover the pastries with plastic wrap or a dish towel and let them rise in a warm place until doubled, about 2–3 hours.

BAKING THE CORNETTI

Preheat the oven to 220°C (430°F).

When ready to bake, brush the cornetti delicately with the beaten egg.

Prepare the sugar syrup. Combine the sugar and water together in a small saucepan and bring to the boil over a low–medium heat to dissolve the sugar. Set aside.

Place the pastries in the hot oven then immediately reduce the heat to 200°C (390°F) and bake for 7–10 minutes, or until the cornetti are golden brown. Reduce further to 180°C (360°F) and continue baking until puffed and evenly browned, another 8 minutes or so. Remove from the oven and place gently on a cooling rack. If the cornetti are darkening too quickly in the oven, remove them immediately and turn down heat or put them on a lower shelf.

Brush the cornetti with the sugar syrup while they are still warm. If desired, sprinkle some raw sugar over the top immediately after brushing with sugar syrup for a bit of crunch.

MAKES ABOUT 20 SMALL PASTRIES

Sfogliatine
SWEET PUFF PASTRIES

250 g (9 oz) plain (all-purpose) flour

1 teaspoon salt

250 g (9 oz) chilled unsalted butter (for the 'butter block')

220 g (8 oz/1 cup) raw (turbinado) sugar

400 g (14 oz) Pastry cream (page 27)

NOTE

Make sure you use a setting that distributes heat equally from the top and bottom of the oven – or make sure you have an oven that cooks well from the bottom to begin with! You may need to place these on a low shelf to make sure that they cook well from underneath; otherwise, you may risk undercooked pastry.

Also known as *borsettine* because they look like little coin purses, *sfogliatine* are available in many Florentine pastry shops. What really makes these special are the crunchy, slightly burnt-caramel bottoms made from rolling the dough over raw sugar as you prepare the pastries. Some are filled simply with pastry cream but others also feature sliced apple, rice pudding (such as in the rice pudding pastries, page 41), jam or even chocolate. You can also keep them flat, somewhat oval shaped and open-faced. Top with pastry cream and cover with thin slices of apple – delicious!

The process for making this homemade puff pastry is similar to the one for cornetti (page 28), but while cornetti dough is 'turned' three times, puff pastry is 'turned' six times.

Place the flour on a board and make a well in the centre of it. Add the salt and 150 ml (5 fl oz) water to the well and mix, slowly incorporating the flour around the water until you have a smooth dough. Let the dough rest in a bowl, covered, for 25 minutes.

THE BUTTER BLOCK

(See 'Making the butter block' on page 30.) Take the butter out of the fridge and let it soften slightly for 30 minutes while the dough is resting. To make the 'butter block', place between two sheets of baking paper and bash it a little with a rolling pin to soften it and shape it into a square, about 12 cm (4½ in) wide.

Roll the dough into a square, about 20 cm (8 in) wide and about 1 cm (½ in) thick. Place the square of butter in the centre of the square of dough at a 45 degree angle to the dough so that the corners of the dough can fold perfectly over the edges of the butter block, encasing it like an envelope. Pinch and seal the dough well. Let it rest for 10 minutes in the fridge, covered loosely with plastic wrap.

THE TURNS

(See 'The turns' on page 30.) The next series of steps are known as 'turns' and consist of folding the rolled out dough into thirds, turning and rolling and folding again. If at any time it begins to get too difficult to roll the dough or the butter seems too soft, place the dough in the fridge and let chill, then try again. For the first pair of turns: roll the dough with a rolling pin on a lightly floured work surface to get a long rectangle (short side facing you), about 1.5 cm (½ in) thick. Fold like a business letter into three: fold the top third down and the bottom third up. Give the dough a quarter turn (90 degrees to the right) and roll to a rectangle as before, i.e. 1.5 cm (½ in) thickness. You may find it harder to roll this time. Fold again the same way into thirds. Let it rest in the fridge, covered loosely, for 15 minutes.

Repeat another pair of turns and let rest in the fridge for 15 minutes, loosely covered. Repeat three more pairs of turns, letting the dough rest in the fridge for 15 minutes, covered loosely, after each fold. Altogether, you should perform six pairs of turns on the dough – this will ensure a flaky puff pastry.

Recipe continued overleaf >

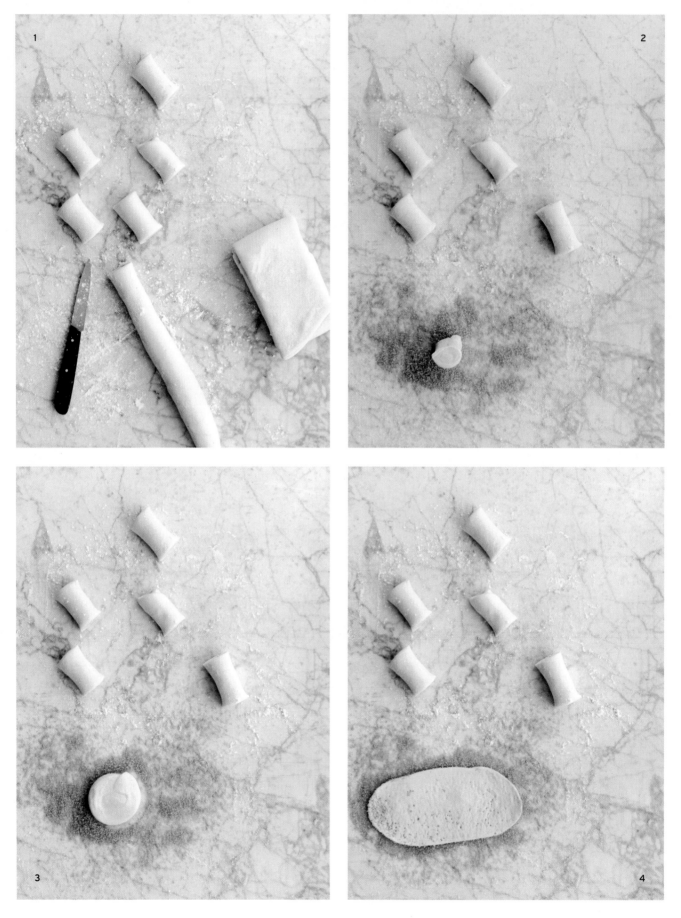

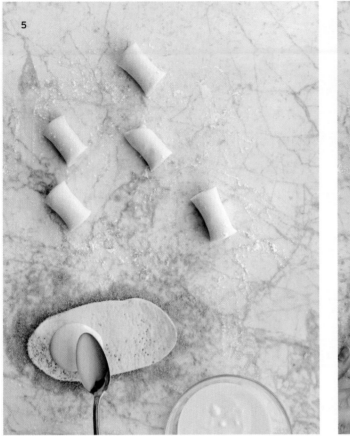

NOTE

These pastries freeze very well. Prepare up until the point of baking and freeze on the baking tray, covered in plastic wrap. When frozen, you can remove the pastries from the tray and store in airtight plastic bags or containers, layered between greaseproof paper. When ready to bake, place the frozen pastries directly from the freezer onto a baking tray and immediately into a hot oven (do not defrost). Bake for an extra 15–20 minutes.

SHAPING THE SFOGLIATINE

Cut the dough into two pieces. Keep one portion covered in the fridge, and roll the other piece of dough out to a long rectangle of 2–3 mm (about ⅛ in) thickness. Roll the rectangle on the short side to create a long log. Cut the log into cylinders 4–5 cm (1½–2 in) long.

Dust the bench top very lightly with flour and sprinkle over a generous amount of raw (turbinado) sugar. Standing each cylinder of dough upright, flatten the dough over the raw sugar with the palm of your hand to create a disc. Lightly dust with flour and roll the disc over the raw sugar from the centre upwards and downwards to obtain an oval shape, approximately 1 mm (¹⁄₁₆ in) thick, 8–9 cm (3–3½ in) wide (in the centre) and 16–18 cm (6–7 in) long.

Place 1 level tablespoon of pastry cream on the bottom half of the oval, brush the edges lightly with water with the tip of your finger and fold the top half of the pastry over the filling. Place the pastry on a baking tray lined with baking paper. Loosely cover with plastic wrap, and continue working each piece of pastry in the same way until completed.

BAKING THE SFOGLIATINE

Preheat the oven to 200°C (400°F). Let the pastries rest in the fridge for 30 minutes, loosely covered. Bake for 10–15 minutes until the sfogliatine are golden and puffed, and the bottoms have caramelised.

MAKES 18-20 SMALL PASTRIES

In the blind treasure hunt that is looking for this place, it's best to just follow your nose (or possibly look out for some other people hanging around an unassuming door); open sometime between midnight and 4 am. Be sure to keep voices down out of respect for the neighbours otherwise the bakers shut the door on you and everyone else waiting for hot pastries!

Secret Bakeries

Without a doubt, one of my best memories of my first time living in Florence as a twenty-one-year-old art student was stumbling upon one of the so-called 'secret bakeries' or *pasticcerie notturne* (nocturnal pastry shops) down an alleyway.

Around midnight, the scent from one of these invisible bakeries would waft up from the street and into the fifth-floor window of the kitchen I shared with a handful of roommates, my wonderful international 'family' for the semester. It wasn't simply the scent of baking bread, it was the smell of hot *pastries*, the kind of smell that instantly made you crave something sweet and baked. I was properly introduced to the source of this tempting aroma about a week after moving in, when my thoughtful roommates, out on the prowl at 4 am, procured a white paper bag of freshly baked cornetti, filled with pastry cream and apricot jam which greeted me in the morning (along with prosecco and orange juice in cocktail glasses) for my twenty-first birthday.

I visited the late night bakery – which is, in reality, a laboratory rather than a shop – many more times myself in the wee hours of the night. With no signs, indications or anything pointing to what looks otherwise like an uninteresting back door down a rather shady, narrow street between the Palazzo Vecchio and Piazza Santa Croce, you simply have to follow that undeniable, magical perfume of butter, flour, sugar and eggs baking.

Patiently waiting outside of that back door, sometimes in freezing temperatures, along with a few other hungry night owls, for the door to be flung open and orders taken – *two cornetti, please! Plain? No, with crema!* – and watching the trays of pastries come flying out of the ovens, two piping hot cornetti pulled off them and injected with still-warm pastry cream, is the stuff of dreams.

Budini *di* Riso

RICE PUDDINGS

100 g (3½ oz) short grain risotto
   rice such as arborio or carnaroli
500 ml (17 fl oz/2 cups) milk
1 tablespoon unsalted butter
2 eggs, beaten
1 tablespoon sugar
a pinch of salt
zest of 1 lemon
zest of 1 orange
1 teaspoon natural vanilla extract
1 quantity Sweet shortcrust pastry
   dough (see page 24)
icing (confectioners') sugar
   for dusting

Many say that the mark of a really good *pasticceria* is their *budini di riso*, a classic breakfast item amongst the line-up at any pastry shop. It's not that they are difficult to do. Actually, they are really quite easy. I believe it's more about the care put into them and the balance of sweetness, as it's so disappointing to get a sickly-sweet *budino di riso*. The short pastry case should be thin, ever so slightly sweet and on the soft, blonde side. The rice pudding should be moist but firm, not hard and not too sweet, as the pretty, powdery icing sugar that coats the top supplies enough sweetness.

To make these, you really only need the classic sweet pastry recipe used for *crostata* (page 24) and the recipe for rice fritters (page 54) minus the flour and baking powder. Simple. To get the right shape, it's ideal to have a friand pan or deep, oval pastry cups. Failing that, you can simply use a regular muffin tin.

To make the rice filling, place the rice and milk in a saucepan over low–medium heat, and cook, stirring frequently until the rice is soft and the mixture is thick and creamy, about 20 minutes (keep a careful eye on it that it doesn't overflow or burn). Take off the heat, add the butter, and let it cool slightly before adding the eggs, sugar, salt, the lemon and orange zest and vanilla. Leave to cool completely.

Preheat the oven to 180°C (360°F).

After resting the pastry dough, place on a lightly floured work surface, and roll out the pastry to a thin 2–3 mm (about ⅛ in) sheet. Cut out rounds and press into eight oval pastry cups or an eight-hole friand pan, leaving a few millimetres (about ⅛ in) of pastry overlapping the lip of the cup. Fill with the cooled rice filling.

Bake the budini for about 30 minutes or until light golden and firm. Let them cool a little in the pan before removing to a wire rack to cool completely. Dust with icing sugar before serving. These are best eaten the day they are made (possibly warm) but you can store them in an airtight container in the refrigerator for a couple of days.

MAKES ABOUT 8 BUDINI

Bomboloncini

DOUGHNUT HOLES

15 g (½ oz) fresh yeast,
  or 7 g (¼ oz/2½ level teaspoons)
  active dry yeast
80 ml (2½ fl oz/⅓ cup) lukewarm
  water
200 g (7 oz) plain (all-purpose) flour
160 g (5½ oz/¾ cup) sugar
30 g (1 oz) melted unsalted butter
a pinch of salt
vegetable oil for frying

NOTE

Don't be put off by frying. Frying is easy. Just make sure to use a pot of oil deep enough that the dough floats while cooking, and be very careful with these bomboloncini as they fry at a relatively low temperature – about 160°C (320°F). To get that crisp, golden-brown exterior and fluffy interior, a sugar thermometer can be very helpful for monitoring the temperature, but if you're not sure of the temperature and don't have a thermometer, simply throw a cube of bread in the hot oil – it should turn golden in about 15 seconds.

The local *bar* near my mother-in-law's house is much like many typical Italian *bars*. People gather there to chat, usually taking an espresso at the counter (standing, of course) or ordering trays of pastries to take home. The coffee's not great, but we don't really go there for the coffee. We go there for the *bomboloncini*. These innocently small, round balls of light, sweet, fluffy dough injected with pastry cream are the perfect mouthful. Somehow, even with an imperfect cup of coffee, that *bomboloncini* makes the morning.

A *bomboloncini* is a golf-ball-sized version of the *bombolone*, the sort of pastry you'd find at every festival or market, freshly deep-fried from the back of a van. Many Tuscans have fond memories of eating *bomboloni* on the beach as a snack but you would never, ever eat these as a dessert after dinner.

Unlike many modern *bomboloni* recipes, which are similar to *krapfen* (northern Italian-style doughnuts), this version is its poorer cousin. It's a very traditional Tuscan recipe that is more like a very soft bread dough deep-fried in vegetable oil. They are pillowy and somewhat lighter than *krapfen*-style doughnuts, which contain eggs.

Dissolve the yeast in the water and let it sit for about 10 minutes. Combine the flour, 50 g (1¾ oz) of the sugar, and the butter and salt in a bowl, and pour over most of the yeast and water mixture. Mix until it comes together. You may not need all the water, but you may need a dash more – this will depend on your flour and environment. Knead the dough on a floured work surface for about 8 minutes, until it's no longer sticky and you have a soft and elastic ball. Put the dough in a bowl and cover with a dish towel. Let it rise in a warm spot away from draughts for 2 hours.

Roll the dough onto a lightly floured work surface until it's about 1 cm (½ in) thick. Cut out circles with a little drinking glass or a small round cookie cutter – I use one about 5 cm (2 in) in diameter. Cut out rounds until you have used all the dough.

Heat the vegetable oil to 160°C (320°F) in a saucepan large enough for the bomboloncini to float (they shouldn't touch the bottom of the pan). Deep-fry in batches of three or four for 2 minutes on each side or until deep golden and puffed. You can sacrifice your first one as a test to check that the inside is fully cooked. If not, you may need to turn down the heat ever so slightly and fry for a bit longer. Drain on paper towel for a moment, then immediately roll in the rest of the sugar and enjoy while still warm.

If you want to fill your bomboloncini with jam or pastry cream, use a metal or plastic tipped piping (icing) bag to squirt a small amount of filling inside each bomboloncino. If you don't have a piping bag, try doing this the way Pellegrino Artusi would have done in 1890 – simply place a teaspoon of jam on one disc of dough, moisten the edges with water, and sandwich another disc on top.

MAKES ABOUT 16-18 SMALL BOMBOLONCINI

Torta *di* Mele

APPLE CAKE

2 large golden delicious apples
(or other good cooking apple),
peeled, cored and sliced 1 cm
(½ in) thick
juice and zest of 1 lemon
180 g (6½ oz) sugar
125 g (4½ oz) unsalted butter,
softened
3 eggs
150 ml (5 fl oz) milk
300 g (10½ oz) plain (all-purpose)
flour
1 teaspoon baking powder
a pinch of salt

This is one of those simple, homely cakes that you imagine everyone's nonna knows how to make and that you will always find, reassuringly, in bakeries, *bars* and pastry shops all over town. It's also commonly on trattoria menus for dessert, although many Florentines would even eat this for breakfast or a mid-morning snack. It's not overly sweet, as Florentines don't have much of a sweet tooth, but you could, if you like, brush a little warmed apricot jam over the top once you take it out of the oven for some shine and an extra touch of sweetness.

Preheat the oven to 180°C (360°F). Grease and line a 23 cm (9 in) cake tin.

Place the apple in a bowl with the lemon juice and 2 tablespoons of the sugar.

Beat the remaining sugar with the butter until pale and creamy, add the eggs and beat very well until you have a thick, pale mixture. Add the milk and the zest, then fold in the flour, baking powder, salt and half the apple slices, along with the lemon juice to combine.

Pour into the prepared cake tin and place the remaining apple slices all over the surface. Bake in the oven for 1 hour, or until the top is golden brown and springy to the touch.

SERVES 8

Torta *di* Semolino e Cioccolato

SEMOLINA & CHOCOLATE TART

½ quantity Sweet shortcrust pastry
dough (see page 24)

SEMOLINA FILLING

500 ml (17 fl oz/2 cups) milk
a pinch of salt
85 g (3 oz/⅔ cup) fine semolina
75 g (2¾ oz/⅓ cup) sugar
finely grated zest of 1 lemon
1 egg, beaten

CHOCOLATE GANACHE

75 ml (2½ fl oz) thick
    (double/heavy) cream
150 g (5½ oz) dark chocolate
    (70% cocoa), finely chopped

NOTE

If you have trouble with the ganache
and it separates, becoming lumpy and
greasy, add a little dash of hot cream
(or even hot water) until it is smooth.

This tart is commonly found in pastry shops as a beautiful, whole tart with
a topping of bittersweet, shiny ganache and a filling of smooth semolina – a
dessert fit to bring to a dinner party or for a special occasion. Semolina or
durum wheat flour is a coarse, pale yellow flour used for making couscous
and fresh pasta (particularly in egg-less pasta doughs). While semolina
used for pasta can be quite coarse in texture, there's also a finer semolina
flour that is used for baking bread in southern Italy. Here, fine semolina
is cooked with milk until it becomes soft and creamy, much like polenta.
When set, it has a pudding-like texture and is the perfect foil to the dark,
rich ganache.

You only need about half the Sweet shortcrust pastry recipe for this tart.
You can halve the recipe (as indicated in the ingredients) or do what I do:
make the whole amount and freeze what you don't use for making mini
tarts or even simple cut-out cookies later.

Preheat the oven to 180°C (360°F).

After resting the pastry dough, roll it out to a thickness of about 3–4 mm (about
⅛ in) and press into a 23 cm (9 in) pie dish, trimming the edges. Place a sheet
of baking paper over the pastry and fill with baking beads (you can also use
dried beans or uncooked rice that you can keep and re-use specifically for this
purpose). Blind bake for 15 minutes.

Take the pastry out of the oven and remove the baking paper with the beads. Let
the pastry cool.

Prepare the semolina by bringing the milk to the boil with the salt. Turn
the heat to medium–low, add the semolina and whisk continuously until the
mixture thickens to a thick porridge (oatmeal) consistency. This should take
8–10 minutes. Taste to check if it's ready – the semolina should feel soft in your
mouth, not grainy. When ready, remove from the heat and stir in the sugar and
zest until combined. When the mixture has cooled, stir in the egg. Spread the
semolina mixture into the tart crust.

Bake at 180°C (360°F) for 40–45 minutes or until the pastry is golden and the
semolina feels firm and springy to the touch. Let it cool completely.

Prepare the ganache by bringing the cream to the boil in a small saucepan. Take
off the heat, add the chocolate to the cream and stir or whisk until very smooth.
Pour the warm ganache over the cooled semolina tart and let it cool completely
to set before slicing and serving.

Store in an airtight container in the refrigerator for up to 3 days.

SERVES 8

Torta *di* Pera e Cioccolato

PEAR & CHOCOLATE CAKE

50 g (1¾ oz) sugar

2 pears, peeled, cored and cut into
eighths lengthways

150 g (5½ oz) dark chocolate

90 g (3 oz) unsalted butter, cubed

90 g (3 oz) caster (superfine) sugar

90 g (3 oz) almond meal

3 eggs, separated

1 teaspoon cocoa powder for dusting

icing (confectioners') sugar for
dusting (optional)

This dessert may be a relative newcomer compared to other local treats but
it is certainly a favourite of Florentines today – you'll find this combination
of pear and chocolate cake in pastry shops and on trattoria menus alike.
Sometimes this cake is encased in a shortcrust pastry too, but I love this
on its own, particularly when it has a dense melt-in-the-mouth texture like
this one. The chocolate part of this cake is modelled on one of my own
favourites: a flourless chocolate cake of Elizabeth David's.

Combine the sugar with 500 ml (17 fl oz/2 cups) water in a saucepan and set
over a medium heat. Add the pear and poach for 10–15 minutes, or until
tender but not too soft (a knife should easily penetrate the flesh without
any resistance). Drain and let the pear pieces cool.

Melt the chocolate over a bain-marie or double boiler. When melted, remove
from the heat, add the butter and stir until the butter has melted. Add the
sugar and almond meal, stirring to combine. When the mixture is cool, add
the egg yolks.

Preheat the oven to 180°C (360°F). Grease a 22–24 cm (8¾–9¼ in) round
springform cake tin and dust with the cocoa powder.

In a separate bowl, whisk the egg whites to firm peaks, then fold them into
the chocolate batter. Pour the chocolate mixture into the tin. Arrange the
pear pieces on the top of the batter, pushing them slightly in. Bake for
40 minutes, or until a skewer inserted into the middle of the cake comes
out clean.

When cool, remove the cake from the cake tin and, just before serving,
dust liberally with icing sugar, if desired. Serve in modest slices – this is
rather rich.

SERVES 8

Torta *della* Nonna

GRANDMOTHER'S TART

50 g (1¾ oz/⅓ cup) pine nuts
1½ quantities Sweet shortcrust pastry
   dough (see page 24)
1 quantity Pastry cream (page 27)
   with the zest of 1 lemon added
milk or water for brushing
icing (confectioners') sugar for
   dusting (optional)

NOTE

This recipe requires 1½ quantities of
the shortcrust pastry. I find it easiest
to just double the pastry recipe and
save the leftovers for making mini
tarts or even simple cut-out cookies.
It also freezes well so you can save
it for later.

This is a classic custard tart that all Florentine pastry shops make. It
requires a few different steps, such as preparing the shortcrust pastry and
pastry cream, but it is actually a very simple and lovely dessert made out
of relatively little. You can substitute slivers of blanched almonds for the
pine nuts if you wish.

Preheat the oven to 180°C (360°F).

Soak the pine nuts in cold water for 10 minutes, then drain. This will stop them
from burning in the oven.

After resting the pastry dough, roll out two-thirds of the dough and line a 23 cm
(9 in) pie dish. Place a sheet of baking paper over the top of the pastry and place
weights such as baking beads (or uncooked rice or dried beans) on top. Blind
bake for 10 minutes, then remove the beads and let the pastry cool.

Fill the cooled pie crust with the pastry cream.

Roll out the rest of the dough to about 2 mm (1⁄16 in) thickness and place over the
top of the tart, trimming the edges. This will shrink a little so leave about 5 mm
(¼ in) extra overhang and seal. Brush the top with milk or water and scatter with
the drained pine nuts.

Bake at 180°C (360°F) for 40 minutes or until the top is golden brown.

When cool, dust with icing sugar (if desired) and serve at room temperature.

SERVES 8

Frittelle *di* Riso

RICE FRITTERS

100 g (3½ oz) short-grain risotto
   rice, such as arborio or carnaroli
500 ml (17 fl oz/2 cups) milk
2 eggs, beaten
1 tablespoon unsalted butter, melted
40 g (1½ oz) plain (all-purpose) flour
1 teaspoon baking powder
a pinch of salt
zest of 1 lemon
zest of 1 orange
1 teaspoon natural vanilla extract
125 g (4½ oz) sugar
vegetable oil for frying

NOTE

It's important to use starchy rice
in this recipe, such as one that you
would use for risotto. The starch
released from the risotto rice ensures
a softer, creamier filling than other
types of rice.

These sugar-crusted, fluffy fritters are essentially deep-fried blobs of rice pudding. They like to say in Tuscany, '*Fritta è bona anche una ciabatta*' (even a slipper is good deep-fried). The Florentines love deep-fried foods, whether it's fried sage leaves sandwiching an anchovy fillet or deep-fried rabbit and artichokes. Carnival time is a special time for deep-fried sweets such as *bomboloncini* (page 42) and *cenci* ('rags' of pastry, deep-fried, page 86).

These frittelle di riso can be found in Florentine bakeries and food vans parked at fairs in February for Carnival, but are perhaps even more commonly associated with *la Festa del Papà* on March 19, Italian Father's Day and St Joseph's Day. It's fitting – aside from being the exemplar father, Joseph is also the patron saint of friers.

Like anything deep-fried, these fritters are best eaten when still hot and crisp. Once cold they turn soggy and the sugar melts away, so cook a batch of these when you have people around and you can share them right away.

Place the rice and the milk in a saucepan and cook over low–medium heat, stirring frequently until the rice is soft and the mixture is thick and creamy, about 20 minutes (keep a careful eye on it that it doesn't overflow or burn).

Remove from the heat and let the rice cool slightly before mixing in the eggs, butter, flour, baking powder, salt, the citrus zest, vanilla and 1 tablespoon of the sugar.

Leave to cool completely and rest the mixture for several hours, or better, cool overnight in the fridge. The mixture should be a little bit runny, similar to pancake batter.

Pour enough oil in a saucepan so that the fritters will be able to float in it, and heat the oil to about 160° (320°F). Drop a small cube of bread in the oil to test whether it's ready – if the bread turns golden in 15 seconds, the oil is hot enough. Drop heaped-teaspoon-sized blobs of rice mixture (measure out the rice mixture onto 1 teaspoon, then use another to push each fritter off the spoon) into the boiling oil. Deep-fry in batches of three or four for 2 minutes on each side (turning them over once) or until evenly deep golden brown.

When cooked, drain the fritters on paper towel for a moment and then roll them in the remaining sugar while still hot. Serve immediately. These are best eaten straight away.

MAKES ABOUT 25-30 FRITTERS

Zuccotto

RICOTTA AND CHOCOLATE FILLED SPONGE CAKE

PAN DI SPAGNA (ITALIAN SPONGE)

120 g (4½ oz) sugar

3 eggs

120 g (4½ oz) plain (all-purpose)
   flour (or potato starch)

FILLING

500 g (1 lb 2 oz) fresh ricotta

75 g (2¾ oz) caster (superfine) sugar

200 ml (7 fl oz) thick (double/heavy)
   cream, whipped (see note)

50 g (1¾ oz) dark chocolate,
   finely chopped

30 g (1 oz) candied orange peel,
   finely chopped

30 g (1 oz/¼ cup) unsweetened
   (Dutch) cocoa powder

SYRUP

50 g (1¾ oz) sugar

65 ml (2¼ fl oz) Alchermes

NOTE

When whipping double cream it's
very easy to overwhip and end up
with a grainy texture, so it's best
to either whip with a whisk to avoid
overbeating or, if using electric
beaters, to whip carefully on a lower
speed until you see it become thick
and fluffy. For those really nervous
about over-whipping but who want to
use electric beaters, add a tablespoon
of milk to the cream before whipping
to help avoid the problem.

Some say this very Florentine dessert of Italian sponge encasing a sweet ricotta filling dates back to the sixteenth century and may have been created by multitasking Renaissance architect Bernardo Buontalenti, who the Florentines also like to credit as the inventor of gelato. To me what makes this so Florentine is its shape – the dome so reminiscent of the more famous dome atop the Duomo. When I see rows of these bright pink domes in pastry shop fridges, I can't help but think of the comparison, but actually the dessert probably gets its name from its similarity to the little red caps worn by priests, which are nicknamed zuccotti.

The pink liqueur that characteristically stains a zuccotto is Alchermes. A Tuscan liqueur that was once touted as an elixir for longevity and used to revive weary spirits, it's now only used in a number of traditional desserts for its colour.

Zuccotto is made in two different ways: it's either frozen and served as a semifreddo (rather like an ice cream cake) or it's simply refrigerated and served fresh. With this one recipe, you can do either and both have good results, but I prefer the latter.

PAN DI SPAGNA

Preheat the oven to 160°C (320°F). Lightly grease a 22 cm (8¾ in) round cake tin and dust with flour.

In a metal bowl set over a bain-marie or double boiler, beat the sugar and eggs together with electric beaters until the mixture reaches 45°C (110°F) and is doubled in size and pale, thick and creamy. This should take about 3 minutes. Fold in the flour, bit by bit, until smooth.

Pour the mixture into the prepared cake tin. Bake for 20 minutes or until golden brown and springy. Gently remove the cake from the tin and let it cool on a rack.

FILLING

Beat the ricotta and sugar togther until creamy. Fold the whipped cream through and divide the mixture evenly into two bowls. In one, combine the chopped chocolate and candied orange peel and stir to combine. In the other, add the cocoa powder and mix until thoroughly combined.

SYRUP

Dissolve the sugar in 200 ml (7 fl oz) water in a small saucepan and bring to the boil. Take off the heat and add the Alchermes. Let cool.

Recipe continued overleaf >

If you have trouble finding Alchermes, a good substitute would be vin santo or another dessert wine (in this case you wouldn't need the sugar syrup as it is sweet enough). Otherwise, use a mixture of kirsch, rum or Grand Marnier. If you are not a fan of candied orange peel, try the fresh zest of 1 orange in its place.

ASSEMBLE THE ZUCCOTTO

Line a deep, medium-sized bowl with plastic wrap. A mixing bowl shape is ideal, about 18 cm (7 in) in diameter at the rim and 9 cm (3½ in) tall.

Slice the sponge into 1 cm (½ in) thick slices. Dip slices on the cut side, one by one, in Alchermes syrup and place a layer of the slices, with the dipped side facing outwards, side by side, until the bowl is completely covered. Brush the slices on the inside with some of the Alchermes syrup. Spoon on the white ricotta cream, covering the bottom and sides evenly. Spoon the cocoa ricotta cream inside and smooth over the top. Place more sponge slices side by side over the top, trimming where necessary, and brush with the rest of the Alchermes syrup.

Cover with plastic wrap, place a plate on top with a weight (a couple of tins of tomatoes, for example) and refrigerate for at least 4 hours or overnight.

To serve, remove the plate and plastic wrap from the top of the bowl and flip the zuccotto onto a serving plate. Remove and discard the rest of the plastic wrap and slice the zuccotto into wedges with a sharp knife.

If you want to serve this frozen, freeze the zuccotto instead of refrigerating and remove from the freezer 1 hour before serving.

MAKES 1 SMALL ZUCCOTTO, SERVES 6-8

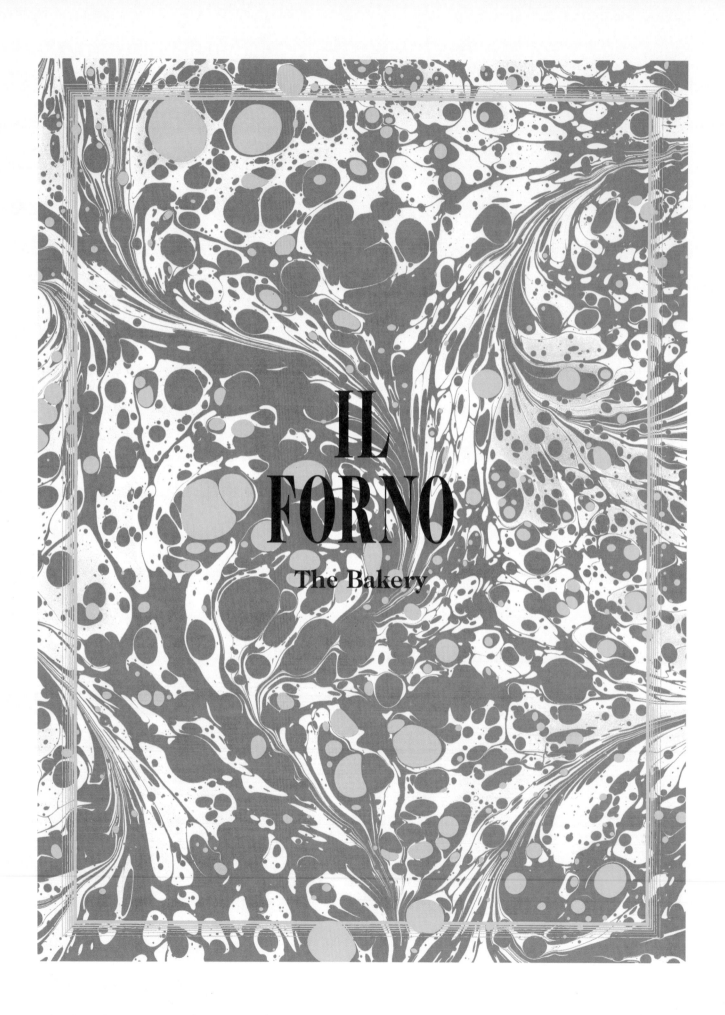

IL FORNO

The Bakery

Schiacciata
TUSCAN FOCACCIA

Pane Toscano
TUSCAN BREAD

Pizza *da* Bar
BAR-STYLE PIZZA

Schiacciatine
VEGETABLE-TOPPED MINI SCHIACCIATA

Cecina
CHICKPEA FLATBREAD

Pandiramerino
ROSEMARY AND SULTANA BUNS

Schiacciata *all'*Uva
GRAPE FOCACCIA

Schiacciata *alla* Fiorentina
FLORENTINE CAKE

Cantuccini
ALMOND BISCOTTI

Cenci
SWEET DEEP-FRIED PASTRY

'The *forno* is the place to grab a quick savoury snack – in particular, schiacciata (plain or sliced open and filled with prosciutto or mortadella) or schiacciatine.'

The shelves of the neighbourhood *forno* (bakery) are heavy under the weight of baskets filled with the morning's fresh loaves of bread, while wide, flat loaves of *schiacciata* (a Tuscan focaccia) lie on chopping boards, where they are easily sectioned. The glass counter has a heaped selection of oven-baked treats, such as almond or chocolate biscotti for dipping into vin santo after meals. Seasonal specialities also feature, such as autumn's *schiacciata all'uva* (flatbread filled with red-wine grapes); and for winter's Carnival, *cenci* (deep-fried pastry with a thick coating of powdery icing sugar) or *schiacciata alla fiorentina*, a simple cake scented with orange zest and vanilla, dusted with icing sugar and emblazoned with a *giglio* (the Florentine lily and symbol of the city) in contrasting cocoa powder. The *forno* is also the place to grab a quick savoury snack – in particular, *schiacciata* (plain or sliced open and filled with prosciutto or mortadella) or *schiacciatine* (small round discs of *schiacciata* topped with cheese, green olives or seasonal vegetables). Some bakeries offer a simple, long, flat margherita pizza, which can be bought by the slice; or *cecina*, a besan (chickpea flour) crêpe borrowed from the Tuscan coast, which is baked in large, hot ovens and served in pizza-like slices garnished with freshly ground black pepper and extra-virgin olive oil. Florentines head to their local *forno* early to get the pick of the best bread before it sells out, or in the mid-afternoon for a savoury snack. This chapter features some of the most popular, traditional Florentine bakery items from the *forno*, delicious treats that are a constant at any of the city's bakeries.

Medieval Florence and the Importance of Bread

Florentines have been making their distinctive *pane toscano* (Tuscan bread) for centuries, at least since the Middle Ages. Dante Aligheri (1265–1321) even refers to it in *The Divine Comedy*. Traditionally it's made unsalted – or *sciocco*, as the Tuscans say, which means bland.

Boccaccio speaks of 'temperate food' in *The Decameron* and bread was the ideal medieval food – perfectly balanced between hot (the wood-fired oven) and cold (the uncooked dough), humid (water) and dry (flour). It was a staple for peasants and nobles alike. Nobles used bread to gather up roasted meat, like an edible extension of the hand. Peasants ate it on its own or, when stale, in soups with vegetables or fragrant herbs – just like it's eaten in *ribollita* or *pappa al pomodoro* today.

Food was generally cooked in just two ways: boiled or roasted. The restored original kitchen of medieval home and museum Palazzo Davanzati reveals how the kitchen's large open fireplace took centre stage – ideal for roasting whole beasts on a spit or holding bubbling cauldrons. Medieval Florentines made thick soups, stews or gruels with millet, chestnuts or stale bread, or whole roasted animals, with meat and vegetables usually cut into convenient finger-sized pieces or even mashed before serving. Much of what was eaten was easily managed with hands or, at the very most, a spoon.

Spices such as cloves, nutmeg, saffron and pepper were an important part of the historical kitchens of the Middle Ages and well into the Renaissance, where they were used in abundance on practically everything in noble kitchens. As expensive commodities, they were highly prized and the use of them was a display of wealth. But other than a status symbol, spices also boosted the flavour of otherwise bland dishes (salt was too expensive) and were used to disguise the unpleasant smell of meat that was past its prime.

Wine and olive oil were well used, and the beating heart of the city was the *Mercato Vecchio* ('Old Market', razed in 1885 and rebuilt as Piazza della Repubblica as you see it today). One of the oldest cookbooks in Italian gastronomic history, the *Anonimo Toscano del XIV Secolo*, survives from this time. It was named for the anonymous Tuscan cook who wrote it and was, most likely, from Florence. Florentine cuisine as we know it today was already taking shape.

Schiacciata

TUSCAN FOCACCIA

20 g (¾ oz) fresh yeast, or 7 g
  (¼ oz/2½ level teaspoons)
  active dry yeast
140 ml (4¾ fl oz) lukewarm water
140 ml (4¾ fl oz) milk, warmed
500 g (1 lb 2 oz) plain (all-purpose
  flour)
2 teaspoons salt flakes
90 ml (3 fl oz) extra-virgin olive oil,
  plus extra to serve
40 g (1½ oz) lard or butter, at room
  temperature

NOTE

You can make this schiacciata using
just water to replace the milk – for a
total of 280 ml (9½ fl oz) water – and
butter to replace the lard. Don't be
afraid of using lard. It not only gives
a more traditional flavour but imparts
a wonderful and characteristic
crunchiness to the top of the
schiacciata.

This recipe makes a fluffy *schiacciata* (a Tuscan focaccia) with a crunchy, golden, oiled top. One of its best features is the dimples created by the baker's fingers as the dough is flattened before baking. They become wonderful pockets for the olive oil and salt, sploshed and scattered liberally over the top of the bread as it goes into the oven. Appropriately, *schiacciata* means 'squashed' or 'flattened'.

A slice of *schiacciata* is a favourite after-school snack, often eaten straight out of the white, waxy paper bag, perhaps after a fight over who gets the *cantuccino* (crust). It is also a popular bread for making panini, which are made on the spot and filled with freshly sliced salumi in good bakeries around Florence.

Stir or crumble the yeast into the water and milk in a mixing bowl and let it sit for 10 minutes to soften. Sift the flour into a wide bowl with 1 teaspoon of the salt and add the yeast and water mixture, 60 ml (2 fl oz/¼ cup) of the olive oil and the lard (or butter). Combine to create a dough. Knead on a lightly floured work surface for about 8–10 minutes until elastic and no longer sticky.

Place the ball of dough in a lightly greased bowl, cover with a damp dish towel or plastic wrap and let the dough rise in a warm place free from draughts, until it has doubled in size, about 1 hour.

Preheat the oven to 200°C (400°F).

Roll or gently stretch the dough out to a rough rectangle. My ideal thickness is 2–3 cm (¾–1¼ in), but you can vary the thickness if you prefer a thicker or thinner bread. Line a baking tray with baking paper and place the schiacciata on top. Dimple the top of the dough with your fingers. Drizzle and/or brush the top with the remaining olive oil and sprinkle with the rest of the salt flakes.

Bake in the oven on the bottom shelf for 20 minutes or until golden. If you like, drizzle with more olive oil before serving.

MAKES 1 LARGE SCHIACCIATA, SERVES 6

Pane Toscano

TUSCAN BREAD

20 g (¾ oz) fresh yeast, or 7 g
 (¼ oz/2½ level teaspoons)
 active dry yeast
300 ml (10½ fl oz) lukewarm water
500 g (1 lb 2 oz) strong flour, plus
 extra for dusting
2 tablespoons extra-virgin olive oil

This is a very simple version of *pane toscano*, adapted so it can be made easily and quickly at home. It's essentially a basic, saltless white bread recipe. Typically, Tuscan bread is baked in a wood-fired oven (it's almost a requirement), which is what helps it get that characteristic hard and dark crust. But if baking in a regular oven, you can leave the bread in the oven, turned off, for an extra 10 minutes after baking for a crunchier crust.

Stir the yeast into the water in a mixing bowl and let it sit for 10 minutes. Pour this over the flour in a wide bowl, add the olive oil and combine to create a dough. Knead on a lightly floured work surface for about 8–10 minutes or until elastic. Place in a lightly greased bowl and cover with a dish towel. Place in a warm place away from draughts and let it rise until it has doubled, about 1–1½ hours.

Dust the dough generously with flour and, on a flat baking tray lined with baking paper, shape into a large, slightly oval loaf. Don't punch the dough down as other bread recipes may require – simply nudge the bread into shape. Dust again with flour if needed. Cover with a dish towel and leave the dough to rise for a further 45–60 minutes.

Preheat the oven to 200°C (400°F).

Bake the bread in the oven for 20 minutes, Reduce the heat to 180°C (360°F) and bake for a further 20–30 minutes, or until the top is golden brown and tapping on the bottom of the loaf produces a hollow sound. When ready, turn off the heat and leave the bread in the oven for an extra 10 minutes to develop a crunchier and darker crust. Remove the loaf and let it cool on a wire rack.

MAKES 1 LOAF

'By far the most important feature of Tuscan bread (and the most obvious, once you bite into it) is its lack of salt. To use the Tuscan word, it's *sciocco*, which means bland.'

Tuscan Bread

'*Un pane più buono ogni giorno che passa*'
A BREAD THAT GETS BETTER EACH DAY THAT PASSES

There are two absolutely essential ingredients in any Florentine kitchen: olive oil and bread. But not just any bread – *pane toscano*, Tuscan bread. As its name suggests, Tuscan bread is used and loved in the kitchens of the entire region, but it is particularly special to Florence, where this humble staple has a very long history. It dates back to at least the Middle Ages, when Florentines likely began making this bread without salt as a result of the expensive cost of this precious commodity.

Tuscan bread is a large, rustic, oval or roundish loaf with a hard and crunchy outer shell harbouring springy, white bread. It has the characteristic of only staying soft and fresh for one day but being useful for many days afterwards, even in its stale state. By far the most important feature of Tuscan bread (and the most obvious, once you bite into it) is its lack of salt. To use the Tuscan word, it's *sciocco*, which means bland.

Dante Alighieri refers to this saltless bread in *The Divine Comedy*, with this quote from *Paradiso*, a moment where he learns of his exile from Florence and is given some idea of the difficulties he'll face: '*Tu proverai si come sa di sale Lo pane altrui, e com'è duro calle Lo scendere e il salir per l'altrui scale.*' In other words, 'You shall learn how salt is the taste of another's bread, and how hard a path the descending and climbing another's stairs.'

For those not used to it, a plain piece of Tuscan bread can be an acquired taste. But it all begins to make sense once you try it the way it is meant to be eaten, with the heavily salted, tasty local ingredients such as *prosciutto toscano* (saltier than prosciutto from Parma, which is known in Tuscany

as *prosciutto dolce*) or *pecorino stagionato* (an aged sheep's milk cheese), or using it to wipe up a plate of *peposo* (peppery beef and red wine stew) or *trippa all fiorentina* (Florentine-style tripe).

This bread's importance is proven even today in the many traditional dishes of Florentine tables and trattorie that would not be complete without this ingredient.

When fresh, Tuscan bread accompanies every antipasto or *secondo* (main); in the latter case it is often used like an extension of your hand for mopping up juices. Charmingly, this is called *fare la scarpetta*, which roughly translates as 'to do the little shoe', a popular, pleasurable way of combining this delicious bread with a meal's tantalising leftover juices. It can be transformed into literally hundreds of variations of crostini after a light grilling, topped simply with a rubbing of garlic and peppery extra-virgin olive oil in its simplest form (known as *fettunta*), or with a classic Tuscan chicken liver pâté. When stale, it can be turned into rustic breadcrumbs, revived in water and vinegar until springy and tossed through a summery panzanella salad, or added to thick soups like *ribollita* or *pappa al pomodoro*.

Stale, saltless bread would be quite useless to most other people, but Tuscans have always been incredibly inventive and good at recreating delicious, hearty meals from yesterday's leftovers, so *pane raffermo* (hardened day-old bread) never gets wasted. I would even go so far as to say that you are likely to find equal amounts of fresh and stale bread in any Tuscan, but particularly Florentine, meal.

Pizza *da* Bar

BAR STYLE PIZZA

DOUGH

20 g (¾ oz) fresh yeast, or 7 g
    ¼ oz/2½ level teaspoons)
    active dry yeast

280 ml (9½ fl oz) lukewarm water

500 g (1 lb 2 oz) plain (all-purpose)
    flour, plus extra for dusting

1½ teaspoons salt

60 ml (2 fl oz/¼ cup) extra-virgin
    olive oil

handful of semolina, flour or polenta
    for dusting

TOPPINGS

400 g (14 oz) tomato passata
    (puréed tomatoes)

15 basil leaves, torn or chopped
    (or 1 teaspoon dried oregano)

200 g (7 oz) fresh balls of mozzarella

extra-virgin olive oil

NOTE

This dough can easily be frozen –
double wrap the portions in plastic
wrap and freeze. When you want to
use it, thaw in the fridge overnight
or on a kitchen bench for a couple
of hours. Let it come to room
temperature before using as normal.

This style of pizza is one that you will find typically behind the counter at an Italian *bar*, that is, a coffee shop that sells pastries and ready-to-go savoury snacks to be consumed right at the counter or taken away in paper bags. Bakeries will often also prepare long, rectangular trays of this crisp, thin-crust pizza with an essential, simple topping of tomato passata (puréed tomatoes) and cheese, cut on demand and sold by the slice. As these are eaten as snacks rather than a meal in themselves, the toppings are quite plain, perhaps with a few simple variations such as the addition of capers, anchovies or prosciutto for those who want a little something more.

This is a quick and easy way to prepare pizza for a party or for snacks. This dough also freezes well (see note).

Stir or crumble the yeast into the water in a mixing bowl and let it sit for 10 minutes to soften. Sift the flour into a wide bowl with the salt and add the yeast and water mixture, and the olive oil. Combine to create a dough. Knead on a lightly floured work surface until elastic and no longer sticky, a few minutes.

Place the ball of dough in a lightly greased bowl, cover with a damp dish towel or plastic wrap and leave it to rise in a warm place free from draughts until it has doubled in size, about 1 hour.

Preheat the oven to 250°C (480°F).

In a small bowl, season the passata with a pinch of salt and pepper, and the herbs. Set aside.

Prepare the mozzarella by draining any excess liquid and tearing into small chunks.

Divide the dough into two even portions. Work with one portion at a time (keeping the rest of the dough covered) on a work surface dusted with semolina (or flour or polenta). Roll and stretch out the dough into a large rectangle (about 28 cm × 25 cm/11 in × 10 in) to a thickness of about 3 mm (⅛ in) and transfer to a baking tray. Repeat with the remaining dough.

Spoon the tomato passata mixture over to just lightly cover the pizza bases, leaving a 2 cm (¾ inch) border around the edge. Scatter the mozzarella chunks over the two pizze, placing them evenly over the surface of each pizza. Position the pizze on two shelves in the oven, one on the lowest rung possible, the other in the middle of the oven. Bake the pizze for a total of 12–15 minutes, swapping them around halfway (this is important to get evenly baked pizza, in particular to ensure the bottoms are cooked). The crust should be golden and crunchy and the cheese melted and bubbling.

Before serving, drizzle the pizze with some extra-virgin olive oil.

MAKES 2 LARGE PIZZE

Schiacciatine

VEGETABLE-TOPPED MINI SCHIACCIATA

1 quantity schiacciata dough
   (page 64)
olive oil, for brushing

ONION TOPPING

1 red onion, halved and thinly sliced
15 g (½ oz) butter
2 tablespoons extra-virgin olive oil
1 handful thyme, leaves picked

TOMATO TOPPING

1 tomato, thinly sliced
1 handful basil, leaves picked

ZUCCHINI TOPPING

2 zucchini (courgette) flowers
olive oil, for drizzling

NOTE

The toppings will cover about
two schiacciatine each.

Any Florentine bakery worth its salt sells these little round discs of *schiacciata* (Tuscan focaccia), sometimes as large as your hand, sometimes slightly larger, sometimes mini versions. They can be baked plain, but more often than not they're baked with a simple vegetable topping – sweet onions, thinly sliced tomato, some zucchini (courgette) or zucchini flowers, or perhaps with just a few green olives pushed into the dough.

They make excellent snacks on the run, are loved by kids and adults alike, and are just the right size for a little afternoon something. Baking them fresh at home is easy and you can vary the toppings as you please – just note that these are always best on the day they are made, so make a batch and spread the freshly-baked love to your friends and family.

DOUGH

Follow the method for schiacciata (page 64) up until the point where the dough has rested for 1 hour.

Flatten the dough slightly on a floured work surface and cut into 8–10 even portions, then roll into balls. Dimple the balls with your fingers, flattening into discs. Line a flat baking tray with baking paper and place the discs on top. Cover with a dish towel and rest for 15 minutes. Dimple again, stretching further. Brush the discs with olive oil and sprinkle with some salt flakes. Cover with the dish towel again and let them rise for 1 hour or until they have doubled in size.

Dimple the discs once more, flattening out the dough until as thin as possible. Brush again with olive oil and top with your selected toppings.

TOPPINGS

Preheat the oven to 220°C (430°F).

For the onion topping, gently sweat the onion slices in a frying pan over a low heat with the butter and olive oil, a pinch of salt and some fresh thyme leaves. Don't let the onions colour – just cook gently until they are completely soft and translucent, for about 10 minutes.

For the tomato topping, simply place fresh slices of tomato on the dough, and sprinkle with salt and torn basil.

For the zucchini flowers, trim the stems to 2–3 cm (¾–1¼ in) long and cut the flowers in half lengthways. Remove the stamen and layer the two halves of each zucchini flower to cover the disc of dough. Sprinkle with salt and olive oil.

Bake the schiacciatine in the oven for about 15 minutes or until golden. Check them about halfway through – if browning too quickly, move to the bottom shelf and turn the heat down to 200°C (400°F). Serve warm or at room temperature.

MAKES 8-10 SMALL SCHIACCIATINE

Cecina

CHICKPEA FLATBREAD

200 g (7 oz) fine besan (chickpea flour)

1½ teaspoons salt

80 ml (2½ fl oz/⅓ cup) extra-virgin olive oil, plus extra to serve

freshly ground black pepper

While not originally Florentine, this is a dish that has been happily adopted by a number of Florentine bakeries. Also known as *torta di ceci*, which literally translates to 'chickpea cake', cecina is really somewhere between a flatbread, a thin-crust pizza and a crêpe, with a crisp, flaky top and almost creamy middle. The smooth, very runny batter is poured into a large round pizza pan so that it is only a few millimetres (about ⅛ in) thick and baked in a very hot oven, preferably wood-fired.

It is a beloved street snack of the Tuscan coast, especially in the area of Livorno, where it is eaten hot with a generous grind of black pepper and a slosh of extra-virgin olive oil and often in between two slices of bread as a panino known as *cinque e cinque*. It's also nice as a starter embellished with some freshly sliced prosciutto or with some garlicky, grilled eggplant (aubergine) slices. It is similar to the *farinata* of the neighbouring coastal region of Liguria, which is sometimes topped with rosemary or freshly sliced seasonal vegetables such as artichokes; or *socca* from Nice on the French Riviera. Clearly this dish was passed on from port to port and developed its own identity in each place.

You can cook this in any shape or size pizza or baking tray so long as the batter remains no higher than 3 mm (⅛ inch). I recommend a heavy tray or pan as thin ones might buckle in the heat, leading to an uneven *cecina*.

Combine the besan and salt, whisking in 600 ml (20½ fl oz) water bit by bit to avoid creating lumps in the batter. When the batter is smooth, add the olive oil and combine. Let the mixture rest for at least 1 hour.

Preheat the oven to 220°C (430°F).

Pour the batter onto a lightly greased pizza tray or baking tray – the batter should be no more than 3 mm (⅛ in) high.

Bake in the hot oven for 20–30 minutes or until the cecina is golden brown, bubbling, flaky and crisp around the edges. It should still have a soft, almost creamy consistency in the middle.

Serve hot, cut into slices, with freshly ground black pepper and extra-virgin olive oil to taste.

SERVES 4-6

Pandiramerino

ROSEMARY & SULTANA BUNS

20 g (¾ oz) fresh yeast, or 7 g
(¼ oz/2½ level teaspoons)
active dry yeast
1 tablespoon sugar
180 ml (6¼ fl oz/¾ cup) lukewarm
water
300 g (10½ oz) plain (all-purpose)
flour, sifted
70 g (2½ oz) sultanas (golden raisins)
2 rosemary sprigs, chopped (about
1 tablespoon)
60 ml (2 fl oz/¼ cup) extra-virgin
olive oil
a pinch of salt
55 g (2 oz/¼ cup) sugar

Shiny and delightfully sticky with decorative split, criss-crossed tops, *pandiramerino*, which means 'rosemary bread' (*ramerino* is the charming Tuscan word for *rosmarino* or rosemary), are little buns fragrant with fresh rosemary and studded with sweet sultanas (golden raisins). Traditionally these rustic buns were made for *giovedì santo*, the Thursday before Easter, and were without the sultanas, hence their name. Now you find them year round in bakeries all over Florence.

Combine the yeast, sugar and water in a mixing bowl and let it sit for 10 minutes until dissolved. Pour over the sifted flour and combine to make a firm ball of dough. Place the dough in a lightly greased bowl, cover with plastic wrap or a dish towel and let it rise in a warm place away from draughts for 1 hour.

Meanwhile, place the sultanas, rosemary and oil together in a bowl and set aside to infuse until the dough has risen.

Combine the dough with the sultanas, rosemary, oil and salt. Work the ingredients together by kneading, and divide into eight small balls, weighing approximately 70–80 g (2½–2¾ oz) each. Place the buns on a baking tray lined with baking paper and cover loosely with a dish towel. Allow the buns to rise for a further 30 minutes.

Preheat the oven to 200°C (400°F).

Brush the tops with olive oil and slash a tick-tack-toe grid (similar to a hash symbol) over each one with a very sharp knife or razor. Let them rest another 10–15 minutes, then bake in the oven for 20 minutes.

Meanwhile, prepare a sugar syrup by dissolving the sugar in 2 tablespoons of water in a small saucepan and bringing to the boil. Take off the heat and brush the hot buns with the hot syrup.

The buns are best eaten the day they are made, but they will keep well for a day or two in an airtight container.

MAKES 8 BUNS

Schiacciata *all'*Uva

GRAPE FOCACCIA

500 g (1 lb 2 oz) plain (all-purpose)
 flour, plus extra for dusting
20 g (¾ oz) fresh yeast, or 7 g
 (¼ oz/2½ level teaspoons)
 active dry yeast
400 ml (13½ fl oz) lukewarm water
75 ml (2½ fl oz) extra-virgin olive oil,
 plus extra for greasing
600 g (1 lb 5 oz) concord grapes
 (or other black grape; see note)
80 g (2¾ oz) caster (superfine) sugar
1 teaspoon aniseed (optional; see
 note on following page)
icing (confectioners') sugar (optional)

NOTE
Avoid using red or white seedless
table grapes or white grapes for
this – they just don't do it justice
in terms of flavour or appearance.
If you can't get concord grapes or
wine grapes, or it's the wrong season,
try replacing them with blueberries.
It's completely unorthodox, of course,
but it's a very good substitute, giving
you a much closer result than using
regular table grapes.

Born in and around the wine-growing areas of Florence and the Chianti, this delicious bread is a tradition governed by the very seasonal nature of grapes in Italy, and one that also has an extremely close tie with the wine harvest in autumn.

For one or two fleeting months of the year from September to October, the appearance of *schiacciata all'uva* in Florence's bakery shop windows is a sign that summer is over and the days will begin to get noticeably shorter. This sticky, sweet focaccia-like bread, full of bright, bursting grapes, is a hint that winemakers are working hard at that moment harvesting their grapes and pressing them. And then, as suddenly as it appeared, the grape focaccia is gone, not to be seen again until the following September.

These days, it is usually made with fragrant, berry-like concord grapes (*uva fragola*) but sometimes you'll still find it made with native Tuscan wine grapes known as *canaiolo* – the small, dark grapes make up part of the blend of Chianti wine, playing a supporting role to sangiovese. These grapes stain the bread purple and lend it its juicy texture and sweet but slightly tart flavour. They are also what give the bread a bit of crunch, as traditionally the seeds are left in and eaten along with the bread.

PREPARING THE DOUGH
This can be done the night before you need to bake it, or a couple of hours ahead of time.

Sift the flour into a large bowl and create a well in the centre.

Dissolve the yeast in about 125 ml (4½ fl oz/½ cup) of the lukewarm water.

Add the yeast mixture to the centre of the flour and mix with your hand or a wooden spoon. Add the rest of the water little by little, working the dough well after each addition to allow the flour to absorb all the water.

Add 1 tablespoon of the extra-virgin olive oil to the dough and combine.

This is quite a wet, sticky dough. Rather than knead, you may need to work it with a wooden spoon or with well-oiled hands for a few minutes until it is smooth. Cover the bowl of dough well with some plastic wrap and set it in a warm place away from draughts until it doubles in size, about 1 hour. If doing this the night before, leave the dough in the bowl to rise in the fridge overnight.

ASSEMBLING THE SCHIACCIATA
Separate the grapes from the stem, then rinse and pat dry. There's no need to deseed them if making this the traditional way (see note).

Preheat the oven to 190°C (375°).

Recipe continued overleaf >

There are rarely adaptations made to this traditional recipe, but often you can find the addition of aniseed – a typical Tuscan flavouring for sweets – as I've suggested here. It's a good addition, one that brings extra perfume to this bread.

Grease a 20 cm × 30 cm (8 in × 12 in) baking tin or a round pizza tray with olive oil. With well-oiled hands, divide the dough into two halves, one slightly larger than the other. Place the larger half onto the greased pan and with your fingers, spread the dough out evenly to cover the pan or so that it is no more than 1.5 cm (½ in) thick.

Place about two-thirds of the grapes onto the first dough layer and sprinkle over half of the sugar, followed by about 30 ml (1 fl oz) of olive oil and ½ teaspoon of the aniseed, if using.

Stretch out the rest of the dough to roughly the size of the pan and cover the grapes with this second layer of dough, stretching to cover the bottom surface. Roll up the edges of the bottom layer of dough from underneath to the top, to seal the edges of the schiacciata. Gently push down on the surface of the dough to create little dimples all over. Cover the top with the rest of the grapes and evenly sprinkle over the remaining aniseed, sugar and olive oil.

Bake for about 30 minutes or until the dough becomes golden and crunchy on top and the grapes are oozing and cooked.

Remove from the heat and allow to cool completely. Cut into squares and enjoy eaten with your hands. If you like, dust with icing (confectioners') sugar just before serving – although this isn't exactly traditional, it is rather nice.

This is best served and eaten the day of baking, or at the most the next day.

MAKES 1 LARGE SCHIACCIATA, SERVES 6-8

Schiacciata *alla* Fiorentina

FLORENTINE CAKE

20 g (¾ oz) fresh yeast, or 7 g
  (¼ oz/2½ level teaspoons)
  active dry yeast
150 ml (5 fl oz) lukewarm water
300 g (10½ oz) plain (all-purpose)
  flour
100 g (3½ oz) lard (or, less
  traditional, butter), softened
100 g (3½ oz) sugar
1 egg, plus 2 egg yolks
zest of 1 orange
1 teaspoon vanilla essence
a pinch of salt
icing (confectioners') sugar
  for dusting
Unsweetened (Dutch) cocoa powder
  (optional; see note)

NOTE

If you want an authentic look, cut out
a paper mask of the Florentine lily
and carefully dust over the top of the
icing sugar with contrasting cocoa
powder. If you want to make this
simple cake a little more substantial,
slice through the middle of the cake
and fill with some slightly sweetened,
freshly whipped cream, pastry cream
(page 27) or diplomat cream (half
pastry cream, half whipped cream)
before dusting with icing sugar.

In February each year, around *Carnevale* (Carnival), there's no avoiding it – the scent of orange peel and vanilla wafts through the cold, late winter air and you can't go past a pastry shop in Florence without noticing that the windows are filled with large, flat, sugar-dusted cakes known as *schiacciata alla fiorentina*. Traditionally served plain, but often filled with sweet, freshly whipped cream or pastry cream, they're instantly recognisable for the *giglio* (the Florentine fleur-de-lis and symbol of the city of Florence), masked and dusted over the top in contrasting powdered cocoa.

This yeasted cake has been a tradition of Carnival season for centuries. With its typical ingredients including lard, eggs and fresh yeast, it would have been a simple, but hearty and caloric country cake. It's directly related, in fact, to the unappealingly but aptly named *schiacciata unta* (greasy schiacciata), which at one time included *ciccioli* (pieces of deep-fried pork fat).

Today's *schiacciata alla fiorentina* is a delicately scented, fluffy, not-too-sweet cake. The characteristic flavour (marked by orange zest) and incredibly soft, spongy texture make it a favourite for a mid-morning or afternoon snack or even breakfast with coffee. It also goes down quite nicely with a glass of vin santo or dessert wine.

Although it requires a long rising time, this cake is easy to make. You could leave it simple with just a dusting of icing (confectioners') sugar. But the hint of bittersweet cocoa goes so well with the subtle orange scent of this cake, you'll want to offer the slice that has the *giglio* on it to your favourite person.

Prepare a rectangular 20 cm × 30 cm (8 in × 12 in) baking tin by greasing and dusting with flour.

Dissolve the yeast in the water in a mixing bowl and let it sit for about 10 minutes.

In a large bowl, mix the flour with the yeast mixture until just combined. Cover with a dish towel and place in a warm, dry spot to rise for about 1 hour, or until the dough has doubled in size.

In a separate bowl, beat the lard, sugar, egg and yolks, orange zest, vanilla and salt very well until the mixture is pale and creamy. Add this to the dough, combining thoroughly until you have a smooth and creamy mixture. Place the dough in the baking tin. The dough should be about 2 cm (¾ in) in height. Cover with some plastic wrap and let it rise for 2 hours.

Preheat the oven to 180°C (360°F).

Bake for 25–30 minutes, or until the surface is firm and golden brown and a skewer inserted in the middle comes out clean. Turn out onto a wire rack to cool. When cooled completely, dust liberally with icing sugar.

SERVES 6

Cantuccini

ALMOND BISCOTTI

125 g (4½ oz) whole almonds,
  chopped roughly in half
350 g (12½ oz) plain (all-purpose)
  flour
200 g (7 oz) sugar
1 teaspoon baking powder
a pinch of salt
2 eggs, plus 1 yolk for glazing
30 ml (1 fl oz) vin santo
1 tablespoon honey

VARIATIONS

The recipe for cantuccini has thousands of variations. While the one I use is adapted from my mother-in-law's recipe, it is quite different from the very first nineteenth-century recipe for biscotti di Prato, which included pine nuts and did not have any raising agents or butter.

If you do not have vin santo on hand, you could substitute another dessert wine or even rum. Otherwise, simply leave it out.

You can replace the almonds with an equal amount of large chunks of dark chocolate (as pictured opposite). Leave the logs to cool completely before slicing and only do the second baking just before serving so you can serve the biscotti warm, with the chocolate just melting.

Tuscan dinners most often end with a plate of almond-studded *cantuccini* accompanied by the local dessert wine, vin santo (perhaps homemade), poured into small tumblers, with much dunking, drinking, eating and lingering. It's the quintessential element that rounds off any meal, whether it is shared among new or old friends at home or offered by friendly and generous trattoria hosts.

In Tuscany they are known as *cantuccini* – often named after Florence's neighbour and the city of their invention, Prato – but they are better known as *biscotti* (the general Italian word for 'biscuits') in the English-speaking world. The word *biscotti* comes from the fact that these biscuits are twice ('*bis*') cooked ('*cotto*'), a technique that Pliny the Elder once said would make baked goods keep for centuries. They are first shaped into a sort of flat log, baked, then cut into slices and baked again. The double baking makes them durable, crunchy and perfect for dipping into vin santo or coffee.

Preheat the oven to 180°C (360°F).

Place the almonds on a baking tray and toast for 10 minutes in the oven, then let them cool.

Combine the dry ingredients in a large bowl. Make a well in the centre and crack the eggs in (reserve the extra yolk for glazing later). Add the vin santo and honey (warmed, if not runny enough) and beat the wet ingredients with a fork, slowly incorporating the dry ingredients around them until it becomes a dough. Add the almonds and continue mixing with your hands until the dough is well combined.

Shape the dough into thin logs, about 2 cm (¾ in) high, 4 cm (1½ in) wide, and slightly flattened. Place on baking trays lined with baking paper, at least 5–8 cm (2–3 in) apart.

Beat the extra egg yolk and brush the tops and sides of the logs with the beaten egg. Bake in the oven at 180°C (360°F) until golden, about 20–25 minutes. Turn the oven down to 130°C (270°F).

When just cool enough to handle, slice the logs at a 45 degree angle into 1.5 cm (½ in) slices (use a sharp, heavy kitchen knife that can easily chop through nuts).

Place the cantuccini on their sides back onto the baking tray, and bake for a further 20 minutes or until crisp and dry to the touch (but not coloured).

These biscuits keep well when stored in an airtight container – if they are not eaten all at once.

MAKES ABOUT 36 BISCOTTI

Cenci

SWEET DEEP-FRIED PASTRY

240 g (8½ oz) plain (all-purpose)
    flour
1 tablespoon caster (superfine) sugar
a pinch of salt
1½ tablespoons olive oil, plus extra
    for deep-frying
2 eggs, beaten
1 tablespoon Alchermes
    (alternatively, use rum, vin santo
    or grappa)
zest of 1 lemon
icing (confectioners') sugar
    for dusting

NOTE

Traditionally these are fried in lard,
which is an excellent medium for
frying for its non-greasy results
(despite what many mistakenly
think). A not-so-fruity olive oil
is the next best choice, but try to
avoid using peanut oil. Alchermes,
a centuries-old Florentine liqueur,
lends the pastry a slightly spiced
perfume but you could substitute
rum or vin santo or, as Artusi does,
even grappa.

Cenci literally means 'rags', which describes the crimp-edged, twisted shapes of this deep-fried pastry that appears in Florentine bakery shop windows during the wintery month of *Carnevale* (Carnival). Many Tuscans get that nostalgic look in their eye when they eat *cenci*, as it's a reminder of dressing up in masks and costumes as a child and biting into these warm, crunchy pastries.

Sift the flour, sugar and salt into a bowl. Make a well in the centre and add the 1½ tablespoons of oil, and the eggs, Alchermes and lemon zest, and beat with a fork, starting from the centre and moving out to incorporate the flour. Finish with your hands to make a compact ball of dough. Wrap the dough in plastic wrap and let it rest for at least 30 minutes.

Roll out the dough on a lightly floured work surface to 2–3 mm (⅛ in) thickness. With a frilled-edge pastry cutter, cut strips of dough about 2.5 cm (1 in) wide and 10 cm (4 in) long.

Heat enough oil in a saucepan so that the dough will float. If you have a sugar thermometer, use it to determine when the oil reaches 150°C (300°F). The dough needs to fry evenly, not too fast and not too slow. You can test with small pieces of leftover pastry dough – the oil is ready to use when the oil starts to bubble immediately, surrounding the dough entirely with tiny bubbles.

Deep-fry the cenci in batches, twisting them or knotting them as you drop them carefully in the hot oil. Cook for about 20–30 seconds per side until a golden-caramel colour. Remove with a slotted spoon and leave to drain on paper towel. They should not be oily or greasy at all, but crisp and dry. Dust with plenty of icing sugar while hot and serve warm or cold with a small glass of vin santo.

These are best eaten the day they are made.

MAKES ABOUT 25 CENCI

IL MERCATO

The Market

Carciofi Ritti
WHOLE BRAISED ARTICHOKES

Piselli *alla* Fiorentina
FLORENTINE-STYLE PEAS

Frittata *di* Finocchi
FENNEL FRITTATA

Insalata *di* Carciofi
RAW ARTICHOKE SALAD

Fagioli *all'*Olio
STEWED CANNELLINI BEANS

Fagioli *all'*Uccelleto
BEANS IN TOMATO SAUCE

Tonno, Fagioli e Cipolla
TUNA, BEAN & ONION SALAD

Baccelli e Pecorino
RAW BROAD BEANS WITH PECORINO

Fagiolini *alla* Fiorentina
FLORENTINE-STYLE GREEN BEANS

Patate *alla* Contadina
FARMER-STYLE POTATOES

Spinaci e Bietole Cotti
COOKED GREENS

Insalata *di* Farro
FARRO SALAD

Panzanella
TOMATO & BREAD SALAD

Fragole e Vino
STRAWBERRIES & WINE

'In Florence, the market is the best place to buy fresh and local, watch the seasons move and see what ingredients are commonly used.'

There is no better way to really understand a city's food and eating habits than through its daily fruit and vegetable market. I have learned a great deal about the essence of Florentine cooking from regular visits to the markets: the strict adherence to the seasons (everything has its time and place, even if it means waiting all year for it), the wonderful simplicity of the traditional recipes guided by the produce, and the little nuggets of knowledge shared above overflowing baskets of long-stemmed artichokes or freshly foraged mushrooms.

In Florence, the market is the best place to buy fresh and local, watch the seasons move and see what ingredients are commonly used – broad beans and artichokes in spring, zucchini (courgette) and tomatoes in summer, fennel and mushrooms in autumn, and *cavolo nero* (black Tuscan kale) in winter. It's also a handy place to pick up tips on the local way to cook this or that, as the vendors or even fellow shoppers are more than happy to impart their advice and even share their recipes. Many of my favourite meals have been ones improvised and inspired by a trip to the market.

Florence is blessed with two large, permanent daily markets, which have been a fixture of Florentine life since the 1870s: the *Mercato Centrale*, the central market in the San Lorenzo neighbourhood, which has recently undergone a very modern facelift; and the Sant'Ambrogio market on the eastern side of the city. Under the one roof, these markets offer not only fruit and vegetables but also butchers, bakers, fishmongers, delicatessens and even stalls and trattorias serving up freshly prepared food. Across the river, in piazza Santo Spirito, there is also a small neighbourhood market held every morning, with a few fruit and vegetable vendors, along with clothing, plants and household items for sale.

Eve Borsook, in *The Companion Guide to Florence* in 1966, paints this picture of the morning market in piazza Santo Spirito: 'At seven the farmers start coming in from nearby hills bringing the freshest of lettuce, herbs, fennel, bunches of flowers, tomatoes, or whatever is in season. Until a few years ago, this was all brought in on red wagons by small donkeys who filled the piazza with the clip-clop of their arrival and departure and hours of their braying conversation ... During the winter there is a frantic race from stall to stall for the best of the Sicilian oranges at the cheapest price, which go by the name of 'Tarocchi' or 'Mori'. The market is the site of the daily convention of the neighbourhood's maids and housewives. Family gossip is exchanged and seller and buyer renew the daily game of needling each other (the produce is never good enough, the price never right). Signora Irma comes with Flick, her small black poodle, girded for battle. The custodian of the coach museum in the Pitti comes to pick up bread and fruit for his wife. Itinerant Sicilian pedlars wheedle odd lire out of reluctant pockets for a handful of lemons and garlic.'

Though it's not quite the same today, and despite its smaller size and offerings, it's still my favourite neighbourhood market in Florence for its genuineness and the people-watching. Gone are the donkeys, naturally, and probably also Signora Irma with her poodle, the museum custodian and Sicilian pedlars of this description, but they've been replaced with other, equally colourful characters – and the Santo Spirito market is still the place for gossip and seasonal produce.

For me, this chapter's recipes have come straight from a visit to the market, arms laden with bagfuls of the season's best produce. Many times, lunch or dinner has been inspired by what looks good at the market stall and this is especially true with raw vegetable dishes such as artichoke salad and broad beans in their pods with pecorino, or salads such as panzanella and farro. When fresh cannellini (lima) beans are available in summer, there's nothing like making stewed beans to have on their own or to use in a number of Florentine dishes. My favourites – *fagioli all'uccelleto* (beans in tomato sauce, page 102) and *tonno, fagioli e cipolla* (tuna, bean and onion salad, page 107) – are featured here. But after that fleeting season, dried beans are reliably always available at the market, stored in large, open baskets, ready to be scooped out and sold by weight.

Although the Florentine menu looks heavily carnivorous, on closer inspection, vegetable dishes abound and arguably are even more varied than their meaty counterparts, thanks to the long-standing availability of good, fresh and plentiful local produce over the centuries.

Carciofi Ritti

WHOLE BRAISED ARTICHOKES

1 lemon, halved

4 whole artichokes

2 tablespoons extra-virgin olive oil

2–3 pancetta slices, chopped

1 garlic clove, finely chopped

1 French shallot or small onion, finely chopped

1 handful of celery leaves, finely chopped

about 150 ml (5 fl oz) white wine (or water or vegetable stock)

2–3 flat-leaf parsley sprigs, chopped

Carciofi ritti (named for the way they are cooked 'standing up') are plump, melting, whole stuffed artichokes, cooked in a simple Tuscan manner until you can cut them like butter. It's the sort of dish you'll find at the height of artichoke season in the most Florentine of trattorie. Artusi even includes *carciofi ritti* amongst his 790 recipes but his version is much simpler, with the artichokes simply stuffed with the stalks and seasoned with salt, pepper and good oil.

These artichokes make a very good side dish to accompany a roast but are equally good on their own as a light meal with some good bread and extra-virgin olive oil (in this case, you may like to double the recipe to have two artichokes per person).

Prepare a bowl of cold water with half a lemon squeezed into it – this is to make sure the artichoke does not oxidise or blacken. Clean the artichokes by trimming the stems as close to the artichoke as possible so you have completely flat bottoms (keep these aside and finely chop) and removing the hard, outer leaves until you arrive at a layer of tender leaves, pale in colour. Don't be alarmed if this has drastically reduced the size of your artichoke!

Chop the top half of the artichokes off completely and with a teaspoon remove the fluffy inside, if present (if they're younger, tender artichokes there may not be any need to do this). Rub the cut part of the artichokes with half a lemon and place in the bowl of lemon water.

Pour the olive oil into a frying pan and place over a low–medium heat. Gently cook the pancetta, garlic, shallot and celery leaves, along with the finely chopped stems of the artichokes, until the vegetables are soft, but not coloured, and the fat of the pancetta has melted.

Gently tease open the leaves of the artichokes from the centre. Arrange the artichokes, cut side up. This is usually done in an appropriately-sized frying pan so they are sitting tightly together and therfore remain upright. Spoon the pancetta filling over the centre of each artichoke and pour enough white wine into the pan to reach about halfway up the artichokes. Bring to a simmer and cook, covered, over a low heat for about 30 minutes or until the artichokes are soft. Test by poking a knife into the side – it should slide in as easily as if the artichoke were made of butter.

Serve with some freshly chopped parsley scattered over the top.

SERVES 4 AS A SIDE DISH

Piselli *alla* Fiorentina

FLORENTINE-STYLE PEAS

60 ml (2 fl oz/¼ cup) extra-virgin
  olive oil
100 g (3½ oz) pancetta, cut into
  thin strips (alternatively, use
  prosciutto or ham)
1–2 garlic cloves, smashed
500 g (1 lb 2 oz/3⅓ cups) fresh,
  shelled peas
4 tablespoons finely chopped
  flat-leaf parsley
1 teaspoon sugar (optional)

NOTE

In Florence you can find baskets of
freshly shelled peas at the market,
which saves a lot of time. You can also
cook this recipe with good-quality
frozen peas with great results.

The pairing of peas and ham is always a good one but the secret ingredient of one of Florence's best-loved *contorni* (side dishes) is a teaspoon of sugar added towards the end. You can choose to leave it out, especially if using sweet, fresh peas, but it adds a certain characteristic sweetness to the dish. The generous addition of water is intentional; the broth that results from cooking the peas is partly what makes this dish so beloved. As Florentine painter-chef Guido Peyron wrote in his recipe book of 1956, '*La grazia dei piselli alla fiorentina è proprio di essere serviti con abbondante aquetta saporosa*,' which means something along the lines of: the saving grace of Florentine-style peas is the fact that it is served with abundant flavourful broth. Like many Florentine dishes, this is even better reheated the next day.

In a saucepan, gently heat 2 tablespoons of the olive oil and cook the pancetta and garlic over a low heat for about 1 minute. Add the peas, parsley and enough cold water to just reach the level of the peas. Season with a pinch of salt and bring to a simmer. Cook until the peas are tender and the garlic is cooked. Add the sugar (if desired) just before removing from the heat.

Serve warm or even at room temperature with the rest of the olive oil, freshly ground pepper and plenty of the broth.

SERVES 4

Frittata *di* Finocchi

FENNEL FRITTATA

1 large fennel bulb, about 500 g
  (1 lb 2 oz)
2 tablespoons extra-virgin olive oil
4 eggs, beaten
35 g (1¼ oz/⅓ cup) finely grated
  parmesan cheese

There's always something to learn at a visit to the market, whether it's just noticing the seasons in the stall displays or the way certain fruits and vegetables are handled. It's also common to get advice on how to cook your selected vegetables by fellow market goers or the vendors themselves. It's a wonderful little exchange of information.

One winter's day at the Sant'Ambrogio markets, I came across an irresistible pile of fresh, bright fennel, spread over a wooden table. Just as I was beginning to gather the prettiest fennel to take home with me, a woman interrupted me. 'No, not that one.' She picked up another bulb of fennel, round and squat, and said, 'This one.' She proceeded to explain that the elongated bulb that I was holding was a female fennel, which was stringy and less flavourful compared to the sweet, rounded male fennel. My fennel dishes have never been the same again.

This is a dish of sweetly stewed fennel in a simple, rustic frittata. You could serve this as part of an antipasto or as an easy lunch or a light dinner, perhaps paired with a leafy salad and some good, crusty Tuscan bread.

Trim the fennel by chopping the tops and bottom off (reserving any green fronds for garnish) and cut the bulb roughly into eights. Place in a saucepan of cold water with a pinch of salt. Bring to the boil and cook the fennel for about 15 minutes or until tender. Drain and let it cool.

Preheat the oven to 180°C (360°F).

Gently heat the olive oil in a frying pan with a heatproof handle. Add the boiled fennel, season with salt and pepper, and pour over the egg, tipping the pan slightly to cover evenly. Sprinkle the cheese evenly over the top and continue to gently cook over a low heat until the eggs are mostly set.

Finish the frittata in the oven for about 5 minutes or until the top of the frittata is cooked and the cheese melted. A nice little crust will form on top. If you don't have a heatproof frying pan, leave it on the stove top but cover with a lid and cook for a further 5 minutes for a softer version.

SERVES 4

Insalata *di* Carciofi

RAW ARTICHOKE SALAD

2 lemons, halved

1.5 kg (3 lb 5 oz) artichokes, roughly
    320 g (11½ oz) cleaned artichokes

60 ml (2 fl oz/¼ cup) extra-virgin
    olive oil

100 g (3½ oz/1 cup) shaved parmesan

When in season, this refreshing salad is often served as an antipasto in Florentine trattorie. The bitterness of the raw artichokes is balanced out by the flakes of salty parmesan and the sourness of the lemon juice. It's a wonderful combination.

Squeeze the juice from half a lemon into a bowl of cold water and then drop the squeezed half-lemon in as well. This is to prevent the cut artichokes from oxidising and blackening.

Clean the artichokes by trimming the stem to about 2 cm (¾ in) and peeling off the hard, outer layer of leaves until you arrive at a layer of tender leaves, pale in colour. Chop the top half of the artichoke off completely, slice it in half from top to bottom and use a teaspoon to cut out the fluffy inside if present (if it's a younger, tender artichoke there may not be any need to do this). Trim the stem of the green outer skin. As soon as each artichoke half is ready, rub with half a lemon and place in the bowl of lemon water. When all the artichokes have been trimmed, slice them as thinly as possible and return the slices to the bowl of lemon water until all the artichoke is sliced.

Drain and pat the artichoke slices dry, then place in a large bowl and dress with the juice of the remaining lemon, olive oil, and some salt and pepper to taste. Toss with the parmesan and serve.

SERVES 4

Fagioli *all'*Olio

STEWED CANNELLINI BEANS

500 g (1 lb 2 oz) dried cannellini
   (lima) beans
2–3 cloves garlic, peeled but whole
4–5 sage leaves
60 ml (2 fl oz/¼ cup) extra-virgin
   olive oil, plus extra to serve
1 tablespoon salt

NOTE

Never throw away the liquid that
beans have been cooking in. Nothing
is wasted in Florentine cooking.
You'll find several recipes call for
this precious liquid, whether to add
flavour to soup or polenta – if you are
not planning on using it right away,
you can keep it in the fridge for a day
or two or freeze it.

It's hard to imagine that beans were not always part of Florence's usual repertoire. So ingrained are they in its food culture that Florentines, and Tuscans in general, are known as *mangiafagioli* (bean eaters). Introduced from the Americas along with tomatoes and potatoes, beans were embraced by the Florentines more than any other ingredient. In fact, Giulio Gandi, in his 1929 book on the characteristic trattorie of Florence writes, 'Beans are the real traditional dish of the Florentines.'

This very simple preparation produces delicious beans, which can be eaten on their own, as a side dish to accompany grilled steak or roast meats, or used in countless other dishes from *fagioli all'uccelleto* (page 102) to soups and salads. In *Italian Food*, Elizabeth David described a similar recipe that she calls '*Fagioli alla fagiolara*', referring to a specially made terracotta container for cooking beans (her recipe includes rosemary and celery). This recipe is similar to the preparation for *fagioli al fiasco*, which was traditionally cooked in an old glass flask of Chianti wine, the straw padding around the outside removed and wound up to make a stopper for the top of the flask. The whole thing was left in the warm ashes of a dying fireplace to cook slowly overnight.

As romantic as a terracotta jar or Chianti flask in a fireplace is, you can get a similar result by cooking these beans very, very gently in a heavy casserole dish for several hours in a low oven or on a low flame on the stove top. The slow cooking will reduce the number of broken beans or skins.

The general rule when cooking beans is that you will end up with triple the weight of the dried beans – so if you want a smaller amount of cooked beans, this recipe can easily be divided. Otherwise, make a big batch and freeze or seal in sterilised jars like you would jam or other preserves and these beans will keep for months.

Rinse the dried cannellini beans and then place them in a very large bowl with plenty of cold water. Leave to soak for at least 8 hours or overnight.

Drain the beans and place in a heavy-based flameproof casserole dish with the garlic, sage, olive oil and 2.5 litres (85 fl oz/10 cups) of water. Bring to a simmer on the lowest heat setting and cook, covered, very gently until the beans are tender, up to 2 hours. Remove any scum that rises to the top of the water with a slotted spoon. Towards the end of cooking, add the salt and some freshly ground pepper.

Drain the beans (but reserve the cooking liquid; see note). Serve dressed in some extra-virgin olive oil as a side dish.

MAKES 1.5 KG (3 LB 5 OZ) COOKED BEANS

Fagioli *all'*Uccelleto

BEANS IN TOMATO SAUCE

2 tablespoons extra-virgin olive oil

2 garlic cloves, smashed with the side of a knife

400 g (14 oz) whole peeled tomatoes or passata (puréed tomatoes)

3–4 sage leaves

500 g (1 lb 2 oz/2 cups) cooked cannellini (lima) beans, either homemade (page 101) or tinned

NOTE

If using fresh beans for this recipe, you will need about 500 g (1 lb 2 oz) of beans in their pods for this. Prepare them as in the Fagioli all'olio recipe (page 101) but they will only need about 45 minutes of cooking time.

Artusi calls these '*fagioli a guisa d'uccellini*', named for the dish that was once prepared during hunting season, which featured little songbirds (*uccelletto* means 'little bird') cooked in very much the same sauce. These beans are a must on Florentine tables, the perfect side dish to accompany hearty steaks or roasts. They are also turned into a meal of their own by adding a couple of pork and fennel Tuscan sausages into the simmering sauce before the beans are added.

In a large saucepan, infuse the olive oil with the garlic over a low heat until fragrant but not coloured. This should only take a few minutes. Add the tomatoes, breaking them up with a wooden spoon if you've used whole ones. Add the sage and about 250 ml (8½ fl oz/1 cup) of the bean cooking liquid (or cold water if using tinned beans) and season with salt and pepper to taste.

Bring to a simmer and cook, uncovered, over a low heat for 10 minutes. Remove the garlic. Add the beans and simmer for a further 10 minutes.

SERVES 4

Catherine de' Medici, a Florentine in Paris

In *The Art of French Cooking*, Ernest Flammarion acknowledges the Florentine cooks in Catherine de' Medici's entourage as the creators of French cuisine. Notable dishes, from *crespelle* (Florentine-style crêpes) to onion soup to sorbet, have been linked to Catherine de' Medici (1519–1589), who was the great-granddaughter of Lorenzo the Magnificent and became the bride of Henry II of France in 1533 at the age of fourteen.

She introduced Tuscan produce such as olive oil, white beans, artichokes and figs, as well as many sauces and desserts. It is said that her favourite vegetable, spinach, was also brought into French kitchens this way, and one story relates that she insisted spinach be included in every meal. The dark leafy vegetable was already well known in Florence in the Middle Ages and by Catherine's time it grew in gardens all around the city. So much was this vegetable connected to the Florentine queen that any dish with spinach in it is still known to the French as 'Florentine style'.

To paraphrase biographer Jean Orieux, the saucepans were overturned with Catherine de' Medici's arrival in Paris.

Not only did she introduce dishes and produce that shook up French cuisine, but Catherine de' Medici is said to have been the one to place a fork on a French table.

Until the sixteenth century, most European table settings included only spoons and knives, often only communal knives. A fork was considered an unnecessary and even effeminate luxury when one had fingers. By many, it was also considered profane. The English word 'fork' and its Italian counterpart '*forchetta*' both come from the Latin word for a pitchfork (*furca*), a correlation that perhaps delayed its entry into table etiquette in the rest of Europe by a couple of centuries.

The first forks, likely used in ancient Greece and Rome, had just two tines, much like today's carving fork. They began re-appearing in Europe via Tuscany and Venice around the eleventh century. It wasn't until the Renaissance, however, that fork-use in Italy was in full swing, with its epicentre in Florence, at the time the most culturally advanced city in the Western world.

Florentine paintings such as Sandro Botticelli's *Nastagio degli Onesti*, commissioned by Lorenzo the Magnificent as a gift for the Pucci family in 1483, depicts the well-dressed guests dining with forks at the wedding banquet of one of the heroes of Boccaccio's *The Decameron*.

But it still took some time for fork-use to catch on in the rest of Europe. In 1611, when an Englishman brought home a fork that he had seen on his travels in Italy, there was wild opposition to its use, and this lasted for centuries. Its pitchfork-likeness caused uproar among clergymen who believed that God's food should be touched only by human fingers.

In France, on the other hand, forks – like Florentine *sorbetto* and other specialities that were introduced by Caterina de' Medici – were initially adopted only by the wealthy, following the Royal French court's example.

With a complete set of cutlery for each person at the table, food could be served in larger pieces, to be cut and eaten delicately. Small bites of food were picked up by the tines of a fork rather than by stained hands. Tables and dishes were forever changed.

Tonno, Fagioli e Cipolla

TUNA, BEAN & ONION SALAD

1 medium red onion, halved and
    thinly sliced
250 ml (8½ fl oz/1 cup) boiling water
250 g (9 oz) tinned tuna in brine,
    drained
350 g (12½ oz) drained, cooked
    cannellini (lima) beans, either
    homemade (page 101) or tinned
2 tablespoons extra-virgin olive oil
1 tablespoon red-wine vinegar
10–12 basil leaves, torn

A satisfying, refreshing salad, *tonno, fagioli e cipolla* is great for a summer lunch or barbecue. Although it is infinitely better when done with dried beans that you have cooked yourself, this also happens to be my go-to lunch when I'm time-poor or have nothing in the fridge, as it can be whipped up in a matter of minutes with good-quality tinned beans and some basil picked out of my herb pots. You could also replace the cannellini (lima) beans with borlotti beans or chickpeas, and the basil with fresh oregano, parsley or marjoram.

To take the edge off the raw onion, put the slices in a mixing bowl and pour boiling water over the top. Let the slices sit for about 5–10 minutes so they are still crunchy and sweet, and drain.

Combine the onion with the remaining ingredients in a bowl with a pinch of salt and pepper, toss together and serve.

SERVES 4

Baccelli e Pecorino

RAW BROAD BEANS WITH PECORINO

20 firm, young broad (fava) bean pods
280 g (10 oz) semi-aged pecorino
  cheese

The first time I properly fell in love with broad (fava) beans was when I learned how to eat them this way. In spring, all the trattorie in Florence will serve this as part of an antipasto. A heaping basket of firm, fresh broad beans, intact in their long pods, is brought to the table, along with a board of bitey pecorino cheese (or perhaps some Tuscan prosciutto). The pods are cracked open and the ever so slightly bitter, raw beans (in their skins) are popped into mouths followed by a salty piece of cheese. It's an ideal pairing for an antipasto – the bitterness in the raw broad beans stimulates the appetite and is a great way to start a meal.

Arrange the pods in a basket, or on a serving plate or pretty wooden chopping board, accompanied by the cheese, sliced or cut into sticks. Supply another plate or basket for the empty pods. Let guests open up the broad beans themselves, eating the beans with a bite of cheese.

SERVES 4 AS AN ANTIPASTO

Fagiolini *alla* Fiorentina

FLORENTINE-STYLE GREEN BEANS

400 g (14 oz) Italian flat beans
   or green beans
1 small red onion, chopped
1 garlic clove, chopped
2 tablespoons extra-virgin olive oil
1 teaspoon fennel seeds, crushed
   in a mortar
400 g (14 oz) tinned whole
   peeled tomatoes
a pinch of salt

This Florentine-style preparation can be used to cook any type of green bean, whether regular green beans, wide Italian flat beans (known as *taccole* in Tuscany, these are my preference for this recipe) or thin snake (yard-long) beans. They sit happily alongside roast potatoes as a traditional side dish to a roast or grilled meat. And like most tomato-based dishes, they're even better the next day.

Rinse the beans and top and tail them. Cut them in half or thirds if very long, and set aside.

Gently cook the onion and garlic in the olive oil in a wide frying pan over low heat until soft and translucent, stirring occasionally, for about 10 minutes. Add the fennel seeds, tomato and salt. Crush the tomato a bit with your spoon. Simmer for 15–20 minutes, then add the beans. Cook until the beans are tender, about 15–20 minutes. If the tomatoes reduce too quickly and become thick, top up with water as necessary.

SERVES 4 AS A SIDE DISH

Patate *alla* Contadina

FARMER-STYLE POTATOES

800 g (1 lb 12 oz) potatoes, peeled
and diced into 4 cm (1½ in) chunks
2 tablespoons extra-virgin olive oil
2 rosemary sprigs
4 sage leaves
1 garlic clove, peeled
400 g (14 oz) tinned whole
peeled tomatoes

This dish also goes by the name *patate rifatte*, or 'redone potatoes', as this is a great way to use leftover boiled potatoes, reheated in a frying pan and served the next day (making them even better than the original dish). These make a good side dish to grilled or roast meats such as *tagliata di manzo* (seared and sliced steak, page 184), *arista* (Florentine roast pork, page 199) or *rosticciana* (grilled pork ribs, page 203).

If you have leftover boiled potatoes, you can skip this first step. Otherwise, place the uncooked potatoes in a large saucepan of cold water with a pinch of salt and bring to the boil. Parboil for 10 minutes and then drain.

Gently heat the olive oil in a large frying pan and cook the herbs and garlic until fragrant. Add the potatoes and stir to cover in oil. When golden, add the tomato (breaking them up a little with your spoon) and 400 ml (13½ fl oz) water. Season with salt and pepper. Simmer uncovered until the potatoes are cooked through and begin to get very soft around the edges, lending the sauce quite a thick consistency.

SERVES 4 AS A SIDE DISH

Spinaci e Bietole Cotti

COOKED GREENS

FOR COOKED SILVERBEET (SWISS CHARD)

2 bunches silverbeet (Swiss chard), about 3 kg (6 lb 10 oz)

FOR COOKED ENGLISH SPINACH

4 bunches English spinach, about 1 kg (2 lb 3 oz)

In delis and even supermarkets around Florence you can always buy prepared, cooked greens – usually English spinach or silverbeet (Swiss chard) – shaped into large balls and ready to purchase by weight and take home to make ravioli, *gnudi* (spinach and ricotta dumplings, page 150) or *crespelle* (Florentine-style crêpes, page 146), to name two typical dishes. They're also rather nice in a warm panino with melted cheese (page 224). It's handy to buy them at the deli but it's also very easy to prepare a batch at home – you can also freeze the balls of greens until you need them.

SILVERBEET

Rinse the silverbeet and remove the white stalks and central vein of the leaves, leaving approximately 800 g (1 lb 12 oz) of green leaves.

Bring a large pot of water (enough to cover the greens) to the boil, add a good pinch of salt and cook the greens for about 8 minutes or until they are tender and dark green. While the greens are cooking, prepare an ice bath. Drain the leaves, plunge them into the ice bath and drain again. If you don't have ice, rinse in cold water instead and then drain. Chop the greens finely and then squeeze to remove as much water as possible. Use as is or shape the greens into two balls and wrap in plastic wrap until needed or freeze.

SPINACH

Remove the roots of the spinach and rinse very thoroughly to remove all traces of dirt. Chop the leaves and stalks roughly.

Bring a large pot of water (enough to cover the greens) to the boil and add a pinch of salt. Meanwhile, prepare an ice bath. Blanch the spinach briefly in the boiling water. Drain the leaves, plunge them into the ice bath and drain again. If you don't have ice, rinse in cold water instead and then drain. Chop the greens finely and then squeeze to remove as much water as possible. Use as is or shape the greens into a ball and wrap in plastic wrap until needed or freeze.

MAKES ABOUT 400 G (14 OZ) COOKED SILVERBEET AND/OR 320 G (11½ OZ) COOKED SPINACH

Insalata *di* Farro

FARRO SALAD

200 g (7 oz) farro

2 tablespoons extra-virgin olive oil, plus extra for drizzling

1 zucchini (courgette), cubed

2 medium tomatoes

1 small red onion, thinly sliced

1 tablespoon red-wine vinegar, plus extra for drizzling

1 bunch (about 150 g/5½ oz) rocket (arugula)

10–12 basil leaves, torn

100 g (3½ oz) fresh *mozzarelline* (small mozzarella balls, such as bocconcini)

NOTE

Some additional ingredients to consider are grilled, sliced eggplant (aubergine), blanched green beans, cherry tomatoes, baby English spinach, olives, herbs such as marjoram or mint, and cubes of young pecorino cheese instead of mozzarella. If you want to make this salad a meal in itself, add some good-quality tinned tuna or legumes such as whole cooked chickpeas or cannellini (lima) beans.

A staple grain of the early Romans, farro is popularly eaten throughout central Italy, in particular Tuscany, Umbria and Lazio, where it's been growing for centuries and has found its way into traditional soups, salads and even desserts.

In Florence, farro salad is a popular lunchtime dish. It makes a delicious lunch for a warm summer's day and is often present at picnics, family gatherings and garden parties, as it's also great for feeding a crowd. It's one of those dishes that you can adapt to the season – just use what's on hand or what looks good at the market.

Cook the farro in a large stockpot of boiling water – at least 1 litre (34 fl oz) – with a pinch of salt. Boil until al dente, about 30 minutes. Check every now and then – depending on the type of farro, this may take a little less or a little longer. Drain the farro and rinse in cold water to cool it down. Set aside to drain and cool completely.

Cook the zucchini in the olive oil in a frying pan over a medium heat until golden, about 5–7 minutes. Season with a pinch of salt and set aside.

Quarter the tomatoes, remove the seeds and chop the flesh. Set aside.

Place the red onion slices in a small bowl with the red-wine vinegar and top with cold water – leave to soak for about 10 minutes to take away a little of the bite. Drain when needed.

Combine all the ingredients in a salad bowl. Toss to combine well. Drizzle with olive oil and red wine vinegar to taste, and season with salt and pepper.

SERVES 4

Bronzino's Panzanella

One of Florence's best-known salads, panzanella (see the following page for a recipe), is usually made these days with ripe summer tomatoes, thinly sliced red onion and torn basil in a bouncy salad, where the main ingredient is crumbled stale bread that has been revived in water and vinegar. It's a centuries-old recipe whose simpler, more essential ancestor of bread and onion salad can be traced back to the Middle Ages with a dish that Boccaccio called '*pan lavato*' (washed bread).

Well before tomatoes were added to this salad, the Florentine painter Bronzino (1503–1572) penned a recipe that almost resembles the modern panzanella. His salad recipe was written in the form of an elegant little ode, where he compares this salad to a trip across the stars:

chi vuol trapassar sopra le stelle
en'tinga il pane e mangia a tirapelle
un'insalata di cipolla trita
colla porcellanetta e citriuoli
vince ogni altro piacer di questa vita
considerate un po' s'aggiungessi bassilico
e ruchetta

(He who wishes to fly above the stars / dip his bread and eat until bursting / a salad of chopped onion / with purslane and cucumbers / wins every other pleasure of this life / consider if I were to add some basil / and rocket)

Native to South America, tomatoes were brought to the Italian peninsula via Spain in the early sixteenth century. Initially the plant was viewed with suspicion and was kept at first as an ornament. It wasn't until well into the next century that tomatoes were used regularly and the Florentines were some of the first, more adventurous cooks to accept this ingredient into their kitchens and vegetable gardens – Grand Duke Cosimo I de' Medici even had them planted in the Boboli Gardens along with other rare and exotic plants when he started his famous Botanical Gardens.

In fact, according to Paolo Petroni in his work on Florentine cuisine, *Il Libro della Vera Cucina Fiorentina*, Florence was one of the first European cities to embrace the unusual foods discovered in the New World after the 1492 discovery – including ingredients such as potatoes, beans, corn, peppers and chocolate. This singular event profoundly changed Florentine and, really, all of Italian cooking, for better or worse. In the *Oxford Companion to Italian Food*, Gillian Riley notes that by the time the tomato had conquered the peninsula it had crept into 'ancient historic dishes which might have been better without them'. I imagine that this panzanella (or Florence's *pappa al pomodoro*) is one of the dishes she had in mind.

Panzanella

TOMATO & BREAD SALAD

250–300 g (9–10½ oz) country-style
  stale bread, ideally a few days old
½ red onion, thinly sliced
60 ml (2 fl oz/¼ cup) red-wine
  vinegar
3 tomatoes
2 small cucumbers
1 large handful rocket (arugula),
  rinsed and dried
60 ml (2 fl oz/¼ cup) extra-virgin
  olive oil
20 basil leaves, torn

This rustic summer salad is a great example of a dish that makes much out of little. It uses inexpensive ingredients and goes a long way to feed a hungry family, all without even having to turn on a stove (a blessing in the sweltering Florentine summer).

Today it is almost always made with crumbled stale bread that has been revived in water, ripe summer tomatoes, crunchy cucumber slices, red onion and torn basil, but this dish most likely began as a simple salad of onion and bread. In the Renaissance, before tomatoes made their way into Italian kitchens, the artist Bronzino penned a poem about a panzanella recipe consisting of cucumbers, basil and rocket (arugula). Actually, many older Tuscans recall having the luxury of fresh tomatoes added to their panzanella only after the Second World War.

This dish is best prepared about an hour before serving to give time for the flavours to combine, but it does not keep well for more than a day as the fresh vegetables tend to lose their crunch in the vinegar. Removing the seeds from the tomatoes and cucumbers ensures that the salad doesn't get too moist. While stale Tuscan bread is able to retain a springy consistency when soaked with liquid, other breads may easily get soggy. Try to find a country-style loaf with a dark, hard crust. Many non-Italian recipes call for toasting the bread, but it is not quite the same as using stale Tuscan bread – in fact, far from it. If you don't already have stale bread, you should dry out (rather than toast) the fresh bread by baking slices in a low oven until dry to the touch, but not coloured.

Remove the crusts from the bread and cut the bread into chunks. Put the bread chunks in a sieve and pass them under running water briefly to moisten. Squeeze out any excess liquid, if any, then let the bread sit in the sieve for 10–15 minutes until springy. Crumble the bread into a large bowl.

Place the red onion in a small bowl with half the vinegar and cover with cold water. Set aside while you put together the rest of the salad.

Quarter the tomatoes and remove the seeds. Chop into 2 cm (¾ in) pieces. Peel the cucumbers, slice them lengthways and spoon out the seeds with a teaspoon. Chop into pieces.

Drain the onions and place in the bowl with the bread. Add the tomato, cucumber and rocket. Season with salt and pepper, and dress in the olive oil and the rest of the red wine vinegar. Toss to combine. Add the basil leaves just before serving.

SERVES 4

Fragole *e* Vino

STRAWBERRIES & WINE

400 g (14 oz) wild strawberries
120 ml (4 fl oz) red wine (such as
    sangiovese) or red dessert wine
1½ tablespoons sugar

NOTE
Be sure to serve this dish as soon
as the wine is poured over the
strawberries. You don't want to give
them any time to marinate as they
go soggy and lose their brightness.

Florentines love fresh fruit to finish a meal and this is a really classy way
to do it, especially when strawberries are in season. Even better, if you
can find them, are wild strawberries, which are commonly found in late
spring in Tuscany – small, sweet and very delicate, they have a melt-in-
the-mouth quality about them.

This dish is inspired by a dessert on offer at one of my favourite Florentine
trattorie, Sostanza, where it is served very simply with a dainty spoon.

Divide the strawberries into four shallow bowls. Pour a quarter of the wine over
each dish and sprinkle each serve with 1 teaspoon of sugar. Serve immediately.

SERVES 4

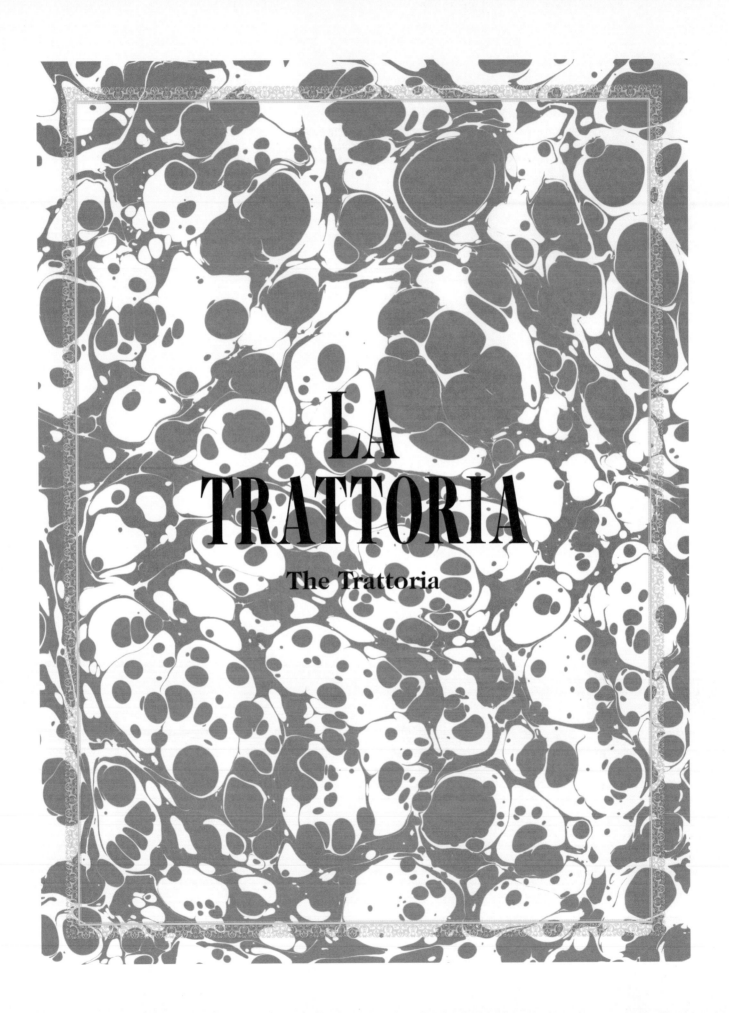

LA TRATTORIA

The Trattoria

Pappa *al* Pomodoro
TOMATO & BREAD SOUP

Ribollita
VEGETABLE & BEAN SOUP

Carabaccia
ONION SOUP

Vellutata *di* Ceci
CREAMY CHICKPEA SOUP

Farinata *con* Cavolo Nero
POLENTA WITH TUSCAN KALE

Crespelle *alla* Fiorentina
FLORENTINE-STYLE CRÊPES

Gnudi
SPINACH & RICOTTA DUMPLINGS

Penne Strascicate
PENNE PASTA WITH MEAT SAUCE

Pappardelle *all'*Anatra
PAPPARDELLE WITH DUCK SAUCE

Topini *di* Patate
LITTLE POTATO PNOCCHI

Ravioloni *di* Pera e Ricotta
PEAR & RICOTTA RAVIOLONI

Sugo *di* Pomodoro
TOMATO SAUCE

Sugo Toscano
MEAT SAUCE

'The lunchtime trattoria is the place to eat a *primo* –
a starter or first course that generally consists
of either a plate of pasta or a hearty soup – tossed
in large aluminium pans by well-versed hands.'

The trattoria is the keeper of culinary traditions, the equivalent of nonna's cooking when it comes to eating out. It offers classics, reliable old favourites that a following of loyal customers depend upon for a weekday meal, a place for nearby workers to grab their lunch. Indeed, the best time of day to experience a Florentine trattoria is a weekday lunch hour when it's all bustle and you're likely to share your table with strangers – some of the most traditional trattorie are still like this and don't even open on the weekends or evenings.

In my mind, the lunchtime trattoria is the place to eat a *primo* – a starter or first course that generally consists of either a plate of pasta or a hearty soup – tossed in large aluminium pans by well-versed hands. Quick and filling enough on its own, but often boosted with a preceding antipasto or followed by a *secondo* (main), the *primo* plays a central role in any trattoria.

The list of *primi* in a Florentine trattoria will almost always include *ribollita* (vegetable and bean soup) or *pappa al pomodoro* (tomato and bread soup) along with favourites like a simple *pasta al pomodoro* (pasta with tomato sauce), *pasta al sugo* or *ragu* (pasta with meat sauce) or its variant, *penne strascicate* (penne pasta with meat sauce). These are essential. There will also likely be a filled pasta such as ravioli, its 'nude' counterpart *gnudi* (spinach and ricotta dumplings) and perhaps even *crespelle*, which are crêpes filled with ravioli-like filling and baked with bechamel and tomato sauce. The seasons have a significant impact on people's appetites and trattoria menus alike. In the cooler weather, for example, a simple, homely bean or chickpea soup may be offered, as well as something gamey like a hearty duck pappardelle – comforting, warming dishes.

Along with these classics, this chapter includes dishes inspired by some of my favourite trattorie, such as *topini* (little potato gnocchi) or ravioli filled with pear and ricotta. Others are age-old recipes that are sadly disappearing off menus, such as *carabaccia* (slowly cooked onion soup) or *farinata con cavolo nero* (a soft polenta with Tuscan kale). Although inspired by trattorias, many of these dishes are also the *primi* commonly found at home. After all, the trattoria's best hits are also the things that mamma or nonna would make – it's home-style cooking, but not at home.

Pappa *al* Pomodoro

TOMATO & BREAD SOUP

1 onion, finely chopped

1 garlic clove, finely chopped

a good pinch of salt

2 tablespoons extra-virgin olive oil, plus extra for drizzling

60 ml (2 fl oz/¼ cup) white wine (or water)

700 g (1 lb 9 oz) tomato passata (puréed tomatoes)

350 ml (12 fl oz) vegetable stock or water

1 small handful basil leaves, torn

350 g (12½ oz) stale bread, cut into slices

An ingenious way to make a cheap, comforting and filling meal, *pappa al pomodoro* is probably one of the most ancient dishes that continues to appear on every single Florentine trattoria menu. As with the panzanella, however, the tomatoes weren't always part of the recipe. This humble dish of medieval origins would have once been a simple porridge (oatmeal) of sorts, made with bread, water and garlic, a dish known as *pancotto*, 'cooked bread', which was described by the Florentine painter-chef, Guido Peyron, as 'the most elemental soup in the world'.

The beauty of a dish like *pappa al pomodoro* is that it is basically a different dish in each house or trattoria, and is made with a slightly different list of ingredients and a different technique. This demonstrates how much this is an instinctive sort of dish, often made with what's on hand and followed without a recipe.

Cook the onion and garlic and salt in the olive oil in a large saucepan over a low heat until soft and translucent, about 10 minutes. Add the wine and continue cooking until the liquid has nearly evaporated. Add the tomato passata and vegetable stock and cook over a medium heat, uncovered, for 20 minutes. Season with pepper and, if needed, more salt (especially if using unsalted Tuscan bread in this recipe).

Just before taking the soup off the heat, add the basil and the bread. Remove from the heat and let it sit, covered, for 1 hour. After this time, stir the soup to break up the bread and adjust the consistency, if necessary, by adding more vegetable stock or water – it should be thick like porridge (oatmeal).

Serve at room temperature in summer or hot in the cooler months, always with a drizzle of olive oil and freshly ground black pepper.

SERVES 4

No Two Alike

There is no standard recipe for *pappa al pomodoro* (tomato and bread soup; see recipe on previous page). The dish morphs as it pans over the different landscapes of Tuscany and, of course, changes from kitchen to kitchen. Some like to use finely chopped leek, others add a few whole cloves or a touch of chilli for added heat, and others use fresh tomatoes instead of tinned. There are also very different techniques used for making this dish, which Tuscans could (and do) argue about for days. The biggest question seems to be whether or not to cook the bread.

The bread is a very sensitive issue when it comes to *pappa al pomodoro*, as it is the base of the dish. It is what gives it its characteristic texture, its volume and, most importantly, it's what makes it a *pappa*, which is the word used to describe a porridge (oatmeal) or baby food or anything else that's soft and mushy.

The bread must be Tuscan, of course, for its great ability to be revived in liquids without turning soggy, and to be a day or more stale rather than toasted. Some simply rub raw garlic sparingly on the stale bread for a delicate, warm garlic flavour instead of adding it directly to the soup. But the most important step of the *pappa al pomodoro* is how and when you add the bread.

I favour the *pappe* made by first cooking a tomato base diluted with water or stock and then, off the heat, resting the stale bread in the tomato mixture to soak up the liquid, only heating it for a couple of minutes at the most to amalgamate it or warm it just before serving. There are also many recipes that involve cooking the soaked bread together with the liquid for 40 minutes or so and the result is a somewhat gluey texture with a thick 'skin' that develops along the sides and top of the soup – some will argue this is the best part.

Ribollita

VEGETABLE & BEAN SOUP

250 g (9 oz) drained, cooked
    cannellini (lima) beans, either
    homemade (page 101) or tinned
1 small brown onion, finely chopped
1 garlic clove, finely chopped,
½ celery stalk, finely chopped
5–6 flat-leaf parsley stalks,
    finely chopped
30 g (1 oz) pancetta, finely chopped
2 tablespoons extra-virgin olive oil
1 tablespoon tomato paste
    (concentrated purée)
125 g (4½ oz) savoy cabbage (about
    ¼ head), chopped
125 g (4½ oz) silverbeet (Swiss
    chard), central veins removed and
    leaves chopped
125 g (4½ oz) cavolo nero (Tuscan
    black kale), central veins removed
    and leaves chopped
1 potato, peeled and diced
125 g (4½ oz) stale bread, cut into
    chunky pieces, crusts removed
1 red onion, quartered (optional)

NOTE

Another flavourful alternative to
using pancetta is the rind of a chunk
of parmesan cheese, which you can
remove just before serving. It also
makes good use of something which
might otherwise get thrown away.

The classic Florentine winter soup, *ribollita*, literally means 'reboiled', which not only implies the use of leftovers but also refers to one of the essential techniques in getting this soup just right. Using stale bread, seasonal vegetables and reliable beans, this is a cheap and nourishing dish.

A key ingredient for this recipe is cavolo nero (Tuscan black kale), a durable, dark green, almost bluish cabbage with long, slender bumpy leaves. At a certain point in winter, cavolo nero seems to be the only thing that you can find in the markets. Florentines use it in many winter dishes: in soups, as a topping for crostini or as a side dish to serve with meat.

Also key is the stale bread, it is what lends the soup its characteristic thickness. *Ribollita*, along with *pappa al pomodoro* and panzanella, is one of the favourite ways to use up stale Tuscan bread – indeed, it's a reason to buy the bread fresh and let it go stale. If you don't have proper, unsalted Tuscan bread handy, use a good Italian loaf, preferably springy and white, with a dark, hard crust.

Artusi's recipe for *ribollita* is, more than one hundred years later, still one of the best ways to make it and every Tuscan household probably does some slight variation on this. This is mine. The way my in-laws (like many Tuscans) like to serve this is with a quarter of a fresh red onion – dip it into the soup and take crunchy bites of onion and soup together. It's not for the faint hearted or those who don't like onion breath but it is certainly an authentic way to eat *ribollita*.

Purée about half of the beans together with about 125 ml (4 fl oz/½ cup) of the bean cooking liquid (or water if using tinned beans) until smooth. Set aside.

Place the onion, garlic, celery, parsley stalks and pancetta in a large stockpot and cook in the olive oil over a low heat. Gently sweat the onion until translucent, about 10 minutes. Add the tomato paste and cook, stirring, for about 2 minutes. Add the cabbage, silverbeet, cavolo nero and potato and cover with 1 litre (34 fl oz/4 cups) water. Season with salt and pepper, then add both the puréed and whole beans. Bring to a simmer, uncovered, and cook until the vegetables are cooked and tender, about 30 minutes – test for tenderness with the poke of a fork.

Remove the pot from the heat. Add the bread, cover the pot and let it rest for at least 20 minutes (but an hour is better). Before serving, stir the pot to break up the soaked bread. It should be thick like porridge (oatmeal) but you can add a bit of water if it is too thick. Reheat gently and serve. If desired, garnish with a quarter of a red onion.

Save any leftovers for reheating the next day. After all, it wouldn't be *ribollita* if it weren't re-boiled.

SERVES 4

Carabaccia

ONION SOUP

1 kg (2 lb 3 oz) red onions, thinly sliced

2 tablespoons extra-virgin olive oil, plus extra for drizzling

4 sage leaves

1 teaspoon salt

4 eggs

75 g (2¾ oz/¾ cup) parmesan cheese, grated

4 thick slices crusty bread, grilled or toasted

VEGETABLE STOCK

1 small brown onion, halved

1 carrot, cut into chunks

1 celery stalk, cut into chunks

1–2 bay leaves

5–6 peppercorns

1 teaspoon salt

NOTE

The vegetable stock freezes well, so it's great to make ahead of time and keep in the freezer until needed.

This Renaissance soup was said to be a favourite of Leonardo da Vinci (who was, apparently, vegetarian). One of the best known versions for this traditional Florentine soup was jotted down in the 1500s by court chef, Cristoforo da Messiburgo, and describes sliced onions cooked in vegetable broth and enriched with ground almonds, vinegar, sugar and cinnamon. Some like to think this was the inspiration for French onion soup, introduced by Catherine de' Medici when her Florentine chefs moved with her to Paris.

Today's *carabaccia* is a mellow, earthier version of the spiced Renaissance soup that relies on slow cooking to draw out the sweetness of the onions. It is extraordinarily humble but it shows how a delicious comforting meal can be made with relatively little. A springtime version includes fresh peas and broad beans, which freshen the soup and add some pretty colour, but I am a fan of simply adding one egg per person, poached in the soup itself.

To make the stock, put the onion, vegetable chunks, bay leaves, peppercorns and salt into a large stockpot with 2 litres (68 fl oz/8 cups) water. Simmer for about 1 hour, covered. Remove the vegetables (or use for something else) and strain the stock.

Have 1 litre (34 fl oz/4 cups) of the vegetable stock at the ready. In a large heavy-bottomed stockpot, gently sauté the onions over the lowest heat in the olive oil with the sage leaves and salt. Sweat them, without letting them colour, to draw out the sweetness, for about 30 minutes. If they begin to get dry or stick, add some of the stock. Add the rest of the stock and simmer for 30 minutes, covered. About 5 minutes before the soup is ready, crack the eggs into the soup, top with cheese and cover, without stirring. The whites should be cooked and the yolks runny and the top covered with melted cheese.

Divide the grilled bread among four bowls and ladle the soup, along with a poached egg, into each bowl, over the top of the bread. Season with freshly ground black pepper.

SERVES 4

Vellutata *di* Ceci

CREAMY CHICKPEA SOUP

300 g (10½ oz) dried chickpeas,
  or about 600 g (1 lb 5 oz) tinned
  chickpeas, drained (see note below)
2 tablespoons extra-virgin olive oil
3 garlic cloves, whole
3–4 fresh rosemary sprigs, leaves
  picked
extra-virgin olive oil, to serve
4 slices ciabatta or country bread,
  grilled or toasted, to serve

NOTE

If using tinned chickpeas, the steps
and timing are drastically reduced.
Follow the step for infusing the oil with
garlic and rosemary. Add the drained
chickpeas, season with salt and
pepper and add water to cover (about
500 ml/17 fl oz/2 cups) and simply
bring to the boil, covered. Since the
tinned chickpeas are already cooked,
from here you simply remove from the
heat, blend the soup until smooth and
follow the rest of the recipe for serving.

Simply flavoured and served with grilled bread rubbed with just a hint of
garlic, this is a homely and frugal but satisfying soup. Much like any other
legume dish, you will get best results if you use dried chickpeas cooked
yourself – I highly recommend to do it this way. But if you want to make
this for a quick weeknight dinner, in a pinch, good quality, pre-cooked,
tinned chickpeas will do.

For a few variations to this easy dish, some like to leave about a quarter
of the chickpeas whole, for added texture, or add fresh or dried chilli for
some heat. To make it a more substantial dish, although not traditionally
Florentine (you are more likely to find this on the coast), it is wonderful
topped with some baby calamari or baby octopus, flash-seared on a grill,
or some steamed vongole clams, dressed with some olive oil, chopped
parsley and fresh lemon wedges.

Rinse the dried chickpeas and soak in a large bowl of cold water for 12 hours,
then drain.

Heat the olive oil in a deep stockpot over a low heat. Gently infuse the oil
with two of the garlic cloves and rosemary for a few minutes. Add the soaked
chickpeas, season with salt and pepper and add water to cover. Use about 1 litre
(34 fl oz/4 cups) water to begin with, top up with water as necessary during
cooking, and use up to 2 litres (68 fl oz/8 cups) total. Cover the pot with a lid and
let it simmer for 2 hours or until the chickpeas are tender.

Blend the soup until very smooth and creamy. If it is too thick, add a little water.
Serve the soup with a drizzle of extra-virgin olive oil, plenty of freshly ground
black pepper and the slices of grilled bread, rubbed lightly with the remaining
garlic clove.

SERVES 4

Farinata *con* Cavolo Nero

POLENTA WITH TUSCAN KALE

1 small onion, finely chopped
½ carrot, finely chopped
½ celery stalk, finely chopped
1 garlic clove, finely chopped
2 tablespoons extra-virgin olive oil
40 g (1½ oz) pancetta, roughly
    chopped
1 bunch (about 250 g/9 oz) cavolo
    nero (Tuscan black kale), veins and
    stems removed and leaves roughly
    chopped
1 tablespoon tomato paste
    (concentrated purée)
1 litre (34 fl oz/4 cups) of vegetable
    stock (if using tinned beans)
300 g (10½ oz) drained, cooked
    cannellini (lima) beans, either
    homemade (page 101) or tinned
180 g (6½ oz) polenta
extra-virgin olive oil, to serve

This warming, hearty, soft polenta dish can be repurposed the next day if there are any leftovers. Simply pour the polenta into a baking dish and smooth over. The next day, the polenta will be set and firm so you can cut them into small squares or rectangles, and grill or fry them and eat them like crostini, perhaps topped with some *sugo toscano* (meat sauce, page 167). This is almost a reason in itself to make a larger batch so you are sure to have leftovers.

Gently cook the onion, carrot, celery and garlic in the olive oil over a low heat until soft and translucent, about 10 minutes. Add the pancetta, cook for a further 2–3 minutes, then add the cavolo nero, tomato paste and stock (if using tinned beans). Traditionally, you would use the liquid leftover from stewing the dried beans, which is thick and very flavourful, so use this if you have it but stock or water can take its place.

Simmer, covered, over low heat for 15–20 minutes, or until the cavolo nero is tender. Then add the drained beans and the polenta, and stir until combined. Simmer, uncovered, for about 40 minutes, stirring occasionally, until the polenta is cooked (it should feel creamy in the mouth, not grainy). Add water if it gets thicker than a porridge (oatmeal) consistency.

Season with salt and pepper and serve in bowls with a drizzle of olive oil.

SERVES 4

Crespelle *alla* Fiorentina

FLORENTINE-STYLE CRÊPES

CRESPELLE BATTER

150 g (5½ oz) plain (all-purpose) flour

2 eggs

450 ml (15 fl oz) milk

40 g (1½ oz) salted butter, melted

a pinch of salt

BECHAMEL SAUCE

50 g (1¾ oz) salted butter

50 g (1¾ oz) plain (all-purpose) flour

500 ml (17 fl oz/2 cups) milk

FILLING AND ASSEMBLY

100 g (3½ oz) cooked, drained and chopped English spinach (about 250 g/9 oz fresh, see page 117)

300 g (10½ oz) fresh ricotta

1 egg

a pinch of salt

a pinch of freshly ground nutmeg

125 ml (4 fl oz/½ cup) Sugo di pomodoro (page 166)

40 g (1½ oz) grated parmesan or pecorino cheese

There is a story that crêpes originated in Florence, not France. *Crespelle* (Florentine crêpes) are not eaten sweet, but are treated much like fresh pasta, somewhere between ravioli, cannelloni and lasagna. They are stuffed with a spinach and ricotta filling, folded or rolled, covered in a generous amount of *besciamella* (bechamel sauce), a few splashes of tomato sauce and grated cheese, then baked in the oven. This age-old dish was once made of crêpes that were no more than wafer-thin egg omelettes, also affectionately known as *pezzole della nonna* (grandma's handkerchiefs) because of their folded form. Today, flour and milk have been added to the crêpe batter, but unlike fresh pasta, which has thousands of different guises and sauce or filling combinations, Florentine *crespelle* are always prepared exactly this way.

The different elements for this dish can all be prepared a day, or even two, in advance: the bechamel sauce, the tomato sauce and the blanched spinach can be prepared well ahead of time and the *crespelle* batter or the cooked *crespelle* can be made the night before. If you are making it all at once, for practical purposes, have the tomato sauce and blanched spinach already handy. Make the crespelle batter and while it is resting, do the bechamel sauce and the spinach and ricotta filling. Once the *crespelle* are cooked, it is just a matter of assembling the whole thing.

CRESPELLE

Sift the flour into a mixing bowl and make a well in the centre. Add the eggs and about 60 ml (2 fl oz/¼ cup) of the milk, whisking from the centre outwards until well combined. Add the rest of the milk and the melted butter and salt. The batter should be fluid (it should run off a spoon like oil) and without lumps. If it is too dense, you can add a little water or some more milk. Set aside to rest in the fridge for about 30 minutes before using.

In the meantime, prepare the bechamel sauce (see overleaf).

To cook the crespelle, lightly grease a non-stick frying pan with olive oil and set over a medium heat. Pour a ladleful of the crespelle batter into the centre of the pan, swirling to form a thin crespella. When the top begins to look dry, gently flip with a spatula and allow to cook for 10 seconds or so more. They don't need to brown; they should remain soft. Set them aside until all the crespelle are cooked.

Recipe continued overleaf >

BECHAMEL SAUCE

Melt the butter in a saucepan over a low heat, add the flour and mix with a whisk or wooden spoon until smooth. Carefully cook for a couple of minutes, stirring constantly. Slowly whisk in the milk until very smooth and bring to the boil, whisking continuously. Cook for 10 minutes or until thickened. The sauce should coat the back of a spoon. Remove from the heat and season with salt. Set aside to cool.

FILLING AND ASSEMBLY

Preheat the oven to 180°C (360°F).

Combine the cooked spinach in a bowl with the ricotta, egg, salt and nutmeg, and mix to combine.

Place a heaped tablespoon of ricotta filling on a crespella, fold in half, then in quarters and place, slightly overlapping, in an ovenproof dish greased with a little olive oil (alternatively you can roll them up like a cigar). Spoon the bechamel sauce over the crespelle and dot the top with a few splashes of sugo di pomodoro. The bechamel should be predominant, just *macchiata* or 'stained', as they say, with the tomato. Sprinkle over the cheese and bake in the oven for 15–20 minutes or until golden brown on top.

MAKES ABOUT 8 CRESPELLE

Gnudi

SPINACH AND RICOTTA DUMPLINGS

350 g (12½ oz) firm ricotta (see note)
300 g (10½ oz) cooked, drained and
    chopped English spinach (about
    1 kg/2 lb 3 oz fresh, see page 117)
2 eggs, beaten
a pinch of salt
a pinch of ground nutmeg
50 g (1¾ oz) plain (all-purpose) flour
50 g (1¾ oz) unsalted butter
20 sage leaves
40 g (1½ oz) grated parmesan,
    to serve

NOTE

If you can, buy your ricotta from
a delicatessen rather than the
supermarket and go for the ricotta
that is usually sold by weight and
is firm enough that it can stand on
its own. This type of ricotta, with
a slightly crumbly texture is closer
to the real thing that you find in Italy.
Tubs of ricotta from the supermarket
have an entirely different texture –
smooth, watery, more like thick
yoghurt – that will affect the result
of this recipe. If your ricotta is watery,
leave it to drain for an hour before
using in a sieve lined with a dish
towel over a bowl. Discard the liquid.

This charmingly named dish means 'nude' and refers to the fact that these
dumplings are essentially the filling for a popular ravioli dish, minus their
pasta coats. They are almost always served in a simple but elegant sauce
of sage and sweet, just-melted butter.

The key to these delicate *gnudi* is to not use flour inside the dumplings,
which can often make them heavy and even gummy. Just a dusting of flour
on the outside helps keep their shape and ensures a fluffy, light outcome.
Prepare these fresh just before you intend to cook them – they do not do
well when made ahead of time or frozen.

Make the gnudi by mixing the ricotta, cooked spinach and eggs until well
combined. Add the salt and nutmeg. You should have a thick, compact mixture.

Place the flour in a bowl. With floured hands, roll walnut-sized spoonfuls of
mixture into the flour to coat and then place on a lightly floured plate or board
until they are all ready.

Prepare a large pot of simmering, salted water and set over a low heat. Carefully
drop the gnudi one by one into the water and cook for about 4–5 minutes or until
they begin to float.

In the meantime, prepare the sauce by melting the butter in a frying pan. Add the
sage leaves and 2–3 spoonfuls of the cooking water and swirl the pan to create a
thick sauce. Season with salt and pepper.

When the gnudi are ready, remove them from the water with a slotted spoon and
place them in the sauce. Turn the heat to low. Swirl the pan gently to coat the
gnudi in the sauce for 1 minute, and serve with cheese.

SERVES 4 (MAKES ABOUT 20 GNUDI)

Penne Strascicate

PENNE PASTA WITH MEAT SAUCE

320 g (11½ oz) penne
500 g (1 lb 2 oz) Sugo toscano
 (page 167)
40 g (1½ oz) grated parmesan

This is a favourite Florentine preparation for an otherwise simple *pasta al sugo* (pasta with meat sauce), found just as often at home as in a trattoria. Penne pasta is a short tube pasta, ideal for this technique as it holds its shape well and the sauce fills the inside of the tube, guaranteeing a tasty bite with each forkful. Initially the pasta is only parboiled and the rest of the cooking is finished in the pan together with the meat sauce, stirring and tossing frequently to avoid sticking to the bottom of the pan. This is actually where the dish gets its name from: *strascicare* means 'to drag' and describes the dragging action of the wooden spoon across the bottom of the pan as you stir the penne through the sauce.

The result is an almost creamy sauce, thanks to the starch released from the pasta as it cooks, and an exceptionally tasty pasta, which absorbs the flavour of the meat sauce as they mingle together in the pan. It is similar to what happens to rice in a risotto and perhaps has inspired the modern *pasta risottata* (pasta cooked like a risotto), but this age-old peasant dish has long been a Florentine classic.

Prepare the sugo toscano (note: you will only need half of the recipe given).

Fill a large pot with water and bring to the boil. Add a generous pinch of salt and semi-cook the pasta over a medium–high heat for about 5 minutes. Drain the pasta, reserving 250 ml (8½ fl oz/1 cup) of the cooking water.

Add the pasta to the sauce in a large frying pan. Cook for 10 minutes over a medium heat, tossing or stirring frequently, using some of the pasta cooking water to loosen the sauce as the pasta finishes cooking to al dente. Towards the end, add the parmesan to finish. Serve immediately.

SERVES 4

Pappardelle *all'*Anatra

PAPPARDELLE WITH DUCK SAUCE

PAPPARDELLE

200 g (7 oz) plain (all-purpose) flour

200 g (7 oz) semolina, plus extra
for dusting

4 eggs

DUCK SAUCE

4 duck legs, about 1 kg (2 lb 3 oz),
skin removed

2 tablespoons extra-virgin olive oil

1 onion, finely chopped

1 small carrot, finely chopped

1 celery stick, finely chopped

1 garlic clove

2 bay leaves

3 sage leaves

½ teaspoon fennel seeds

80 g (2¾ oz) pancetta (or prosciutto)

500 ml (17 fl oz/2 cups) red wine

400 g (14 oz) tomato passata
(puréed tomatoes)

grated parmesan, to serve (optional)

Florentines love fresh pasta and, in particular, *pappardelle* – wide, flat noodles often made with a ruffled edge that cleverly holds sauce. It is the ideal accompaniment to rich, gamey Tuscan sauces of wild boar, venison, duck or hare. The word *pappardelle* comes from '*pappare*' (where the word '*pappa*' also stems from), which roughly translates as 'to devour', an apt description for how best to enjoy this pasta.

Traditionally made with a whole duck, carcass and all, this dish is quite extraordinary and incredibly flavourful. You can imagine that in times past, a whole duck was probably easier to get than four duck legs, which might seem quite wasteful. There are many Tuscans (such as my husband's relatives) who are lucky enough to have a bit of land and who still rear their own ducks for food. Using the whole bird in a recipe like this is a way to make the most out of what you have and not waste a thing, while creating the best possible flavour.

I like this dish the traditional way, using a whole duck; but buying a whole duck for this purpose may be a bit expensive. Another option is to just use the duck legs, as I have done here. You'll have a bit more meat this way and the bones still lend good flavour to the sauce.

PAPPARDELLE

Sift the flour and semolina onto a flat work surface and create a well in the middle with your hands. Crack the eggs into the well. Gently beat the eggs with a fork in a circular motion until they become creamy. Begin incorporating the flour and semolina little by little until it becomes too difficult to use the fork and then gather the dough with your hands. Knead for about 10 minutes or until it becomes elastic. Let the dough rest, covered so it does not dry out, for at least 30 minutes.

Divide the dough into two or three portions. With a pasta rolling machine or a rolling pin on a floured surface, roll out the dough until about 1 mm (1⁄16 in) thick or until you can see your fingers through the other side. If rolling by hand, roll from the centre outwards.

The noodles should be cut to about 2–2.5 cm (¾–1 in) wide. Fold the dough lengthways over itself three or four times (dust with semolina between each fold so they do not stick) and then cut across the short side of the folded pasta. Use a sharp knife for a straight edge or a fluted pastry wheel cutter for a ruffled effect (good for catching sauce). Unroll the pasta, shaking it out, dust generously with semolina and shape into little 'nests' of equal portions – 100 g (3½ oz) is equal to one serving. Cover under a dish towel or plastic wrap until ready to use.

Recipe continued overleaf >

If you are not planning on using the pasta immediately, freeze for later use or keep it in the refrigerator in an airtight container for 2–3 days. Try not to squash the nest shapes, they should help keep the noodles from sticking to each other.

DUCK SAUCE

Brown the duck legs in a large casserole pot with the olive oil over a medium heat. This should take about 5 minutes on each side. Remove from the pot and set aside. Drain any excess fat and add the vegetables, garlic, herbs, fennel seeds and pancetta. Season with salt and pepper. Let the mixture sweat over a gentle heat, stirring occasionally. When the vegetables are soft but not browned, add the wine and return the duck to the pan. Simmer, covered, for 1½–2 hours or until the meat is very tender.

Remove the duck legs from the pot and strip the meat off the bone. Discard the bones and chop or shred the meat. Return to the pot. Add the tomato passata along with 125 ml (4 fl oz/½ cup) of water. Bring to a simmer over low–medium heat and let the sauce reduce, uncovered, until thick. This should take about 20–30 minutes.

Cook the pasta in boiling, salted water for about 3–5 minutes, or until silky and cooked al dente. Drain and add to the warm sauce. Toss until well coated and serve, if desired, with some grated parmesan.

SERVES 4

Topini *di* Patate

LITTLE POTATO GNOCCHI

1 kg (2 lb 3 oz) potatoes of similar
 size (use a starchy variety such
 as Dutch creams, king edward
 or Idaho russet)
a pinch of salt
1 egg, beaten
250 g (9 oz) plain (all-purpose) flour

These little round potato gnocchi are called *topini* in Florence (an unusual name as *topini* means 'mice'). Instead of the traditional ridged, rectangular pillows, these gnocchi are simply small balls, which means they are very easy to make. They are usually served with either *sugo toscano* (meat sauce, page 167) or *sugo di pomodoro* (tomato sauce, page 166), or simply with melted butter and grated parmesan. In the summer, these are lovely with chopped fresh tomatoes and perhaps a dollop of pesto.

The secret to light and fluffy gnocchi begins with the right potato and the right proportion of flour – the less moisture in the potatoes, the less flour you have to add, which means lighter gnocchi. Too much flour will contribute to unpleasantly chewy gnocchi. In Italy, you will often see recipes calling for 'old potatoes'. The idea behind this is that old potatoes have a lower water content. Similarly, the more starchy the potato (such as those good for mashing), the less flour you will need. In this recipe, the process is all about removing as much moisture as possible from the potatoes to ensure pillowy gnocchi. Potatoes are boiled whole, in their skins, which means less moisture penetrates them. They are peeled and mashed while still hot, then spread out to release as much steam as possible, resulting in a dry, fluffy mixture. This is mixed with only as much flour as needed to obtain a smooth dough and it is worked as little as possible so that the dough won't become tough. Now you're on your way to ideal gnocchi – or in this case, *topini*.

Rinse the potatoes and put them in a pot of cold water, skins on and whole. Bring to the boil and cook until a fork easily slips into them. Drain and peel the skins while still hot (use a fork to 'hold' the potato for you in one hand while you peel the skin with a sharp knife using the other hand). Immediately put them through a potato ricer or mash them, add the salt and spread out over a chopping board or a tray to allow the steam to escape as quickly as possible.

When cool, add the egg and mix to combine. Add the flour, bit by bit, incorporating with each addition until no longer sticky and you have a smooth and easy-to-handle dough, and then stop (you may or may not need all of the flour). The dough should be neither sticky nor crumbly and the mixture should not be worked too much.

On a lightly floured work surface, cut the dough into four portions. Work with one piece at a time (rest the other pieces under a tea or dish towel), roll the dough into a long log about 1.5–2 cm (½–¾ in) thick. Cut into pieces 1.5 cm (½ in) long and roll these pieces into small balls. Continue until the dough is finished.

Cook the topini in a large saucepan of gently simmering, salted water over a low heat until they begin to float. Remove gently with a slotted spoon and serve with your preferred sauce.

SERVES 4

Ravioloni *di* Pera e Ricotta

PEAR & RICOTTA RAVIOLONI

grated pecorino cheese, to serve

PASTA

400 g (14 oz) plain (all-purpose) flour

2 eggs, plus 4 yolks (reserve 1 egg
 white for later)

FILLING

2 medium pears, peeled, cored
 and quartered

200 g (7 oz) ricotta

80 g (2¾ oz) grated pecorino cheese

1 egg yolk

a pinch of salt

SAUCE

50 g (1¾ oz) salted butter

8 sage leaves

Ravioloni are simply large ravioli. This is a variation on the more classic spinach and ricotta ravioli, which is commonly served very simply with a butter and sage sauce (similar to *gnudi*). It is inspired by a dish from a popular Florentine restaurant, comprising little pasta bundles filled with pear in a cheese sauce. The pairing of pear with pecorino cheese is a favourite, whether it's fresh fruit on a cheese platter, on crostini or in some other form.

Although the classic pasta ratio is 1 whole egg per 100 g (3½ oz) of flour, this pasta recipe uses yolks to replace some of the whole eggs because the whites of the eggs tend to make pasta puff up when cooked – this is undesirable for filled pasta such as ravioli because you are aiming for the thinnest pasta achievable for the best results, both in terms of visual appeal and bite.

PASTA

Put the flour in a bowl and make a well in the centre. Put the eggs, yolks and 2 tablespoons water in the well. With a fork, begin to whisk the eggs, incorporating the flour little by little until you can no longer whisk with the fork. Use floured hands to combine the rest of the flour and knead for about 5 minutes or until you have a smooth, elastic dough (to tell if it is elastic, it should bounce back when poked). Wrap in plastic wrap and let it rest for at least 30 minutes.

FILLING

Poach the pear quarters in a saucepan of boiling water until just tender, about 10 minutes. Drain and let them cool, then chop into tiny pieces. Combine the pears with the rest of the filling ingredients. Chill until needed.

RAVIOLONI

Cut the dough into four pieces and dust lightly with flour. Roll out the dough using a pasta machine, working down one by one to the narrower settings, or with a rolling pin. The dough should be thin enough so that you can see your hand through it. If rolling by hand, you will notice this is a very elastic dough and tends to bounce back – roll from the centre outwards.

Recipe continued overleaf ›

Working on strips of pasta at least 10 cm (4 in) wide and as long as you like, place 1 teaspoon of filling onto the pasta sheet about 5 cm (2 in) apart. Beat the leftover egg white from earlier and brush it all around the filling. Then place a sheet of pasta of the same width and length over the top and, working quickly, press the pasta sheet down carefully around each spoonful of filling, being careful not to trap too much air. Work from one side to the other and, if needed (and if you have two extra hands helping you), work one ravioloni at a time. With a fluted pastry wheel cutter or a sharp knife, trim the ravioloni so that you have a 1 cm (½ in) border around the filling (you can save the trimmed pieces, knead them together and keep using – cover when not in use to avoid drying). Continue until you finish the pasta and the filling.

Cook the ravioloni immediately in a saucepan of salted, boiling water over a medium heat until al dente, about 5 minutes.

In the meantime, make the sauce by melting the butter in a large frying pan over a medium heat. Add the sage and a ladleful of the pasta cooking water and swirl in the pan – this will create an emulsion, a slightly thicker sauce.

When the ravioloni are ready, drain them with a slotted spoon, add to the sauce and toss gently to coat. Serve the ravioloni with the sauce and some grated pecorino cheese.

SERVES 4

Sugo *di* Pomodoro

TOMATO SAUCE

1 onion, finely chopped
a pinch of salt
1 tablespoon extra-virgin olive oil
1 garlic clove, finely chopped
10 basil leaves
700 g (1 lb 9 oz) tomato passata
  (puréed tomatoes)

This is a basic sauce that can dress ravioli, *topini* (little potato gnocchi, page 160) and *gnudi* (spinach and ricotta dumplings, page 150), or even a humble *pasta al pomodoro*. Use this also as the sauce for crumbed meat fillets in *braciole rifatte* (crumbed beef in tomato sauce, page 190) and for 'staining' the top of *crespelle alla fiorentina* (Florentine-style crêpes, page 146) before they hit the oven. You may not need the entire amount but this will store well, in a jar, in the fridge for several days, or you can easily halve the recipe. The longer you cook this, the tastier it gets.

Gently sauté the onion with the salt and olive oil in a frying pan over a low heat. When soft and translucent, add the garlic and cook for a further 5 minutes. Add the basil and then immediately pour over the tomato passata and 500 ml (17 fl oz/2 cups) water and let it simmer, uncovered, until reduced and thick. This should take a minimum of 30–40 minutes and up to 2 hours, depending on how thick you like it. Season to taste with salt and pepper.

MAKES 850 G (1 LB 14 OZ)

Sugo Toscano

MEAT SAUCE

2 tablespoons extra-virgin olive oil

500 g (1 lb 2 oz) minced (ground) beef

1 celery stalk, finely chopped

1 carrot, finely chopped

1 brown onion, finely chopped

1 tablespoon tomato paste (concentrated purée)

500 ml (17 fl oz/2 cups) red or white wine

325 g (11½ oz) tomato passata (puréed tomatoes)

This is my husband Marco's recipe for meat sauce or ragù, which is also simply called *sugo* ('sauce') in Tuscany – the main ingredient for a good *sugo*, they say, is time. The longer you can cook it, the better it will be, so put it on your lowest heat setting and keep an eye on it. Use this to dress *topini* (little potato gnocchi, page 160), pappardelle, ravioli or your favourite pasta. It's also great atop polenta crostini (page 144). Any leftovers can be revived in *penne strascicate* (penne pasta with meat sauce, page 153).

Heat the olive oil in a large, heavy-bottomed stockpot over a medium–high heat. Brown the meat for about 10–15 minutes. When cooked, remove it from the pot and set aside for later. Add the chopped vegetables to the pot and turn the heat to low. Season with salt and pepper and gently sweat the vegetables until soft but not browned. Cook gently, stirring occasionally, for about 20 minutes. Return the meat to the pot, add the tomato paste and cook, stirring, for a minute or two. Cover with the wine and cook, uncovered, until the wine has reduced almost completely.

Add the tomato passata and about 325 ml (11 fl oz) water. Season to taste with salt and pepper. Bring to a gentle simmer and let it cook on the lowest heat possible, covered, for 2–3 hours. Check and stir every now and then; you may need to top it up with water if it is getting too dry too quickly. If not using all of it at once, you can store in an air-tight container in the fridge for several days. It also freezes well.

MAKES ABOUT 1 KG (2 LB 3 OZ)

IL MACCELLAIO

The Butcher

Crostini *di* Fegatini
CHICKEN LIVER PÂTÉ CROSTINI

Pollo *al* Mattone
CHICKEN COOKED UNDER A BRICK

Pollo Fritto *alla* Fiorentina
FLORENTINE FRIED CHICKEN

Polpette *di* Trippa
TRIPE MEATBALLS

Coniglio *con le* Olive
RABBIT & OLIVE STEW

Tagliata *di* Manzo
SEARED & SLICED STEAK

Bistecca *alla* Fiorentina
FLORENTINE STEAK

Braciole Rifatte
CRUMBED BEEF IN TOMATO SAUCE

Fegatelli *di* Maiale
PORK LIVER PARCELS

Trippa *alla* Fiorentina
FLORENTINE-STYLE TRIPE

Arista *di* Maiale
FLORENTINE ROAST PORK

Polpettone *alla* Fiorentina
FLORENTINE MEATLOAF

Rosticciana
GRILLED PORK RIBS

Peposo
BEEF & PEPPER STEW

Whenever anyone asks me about the most quintessential Florentine dish, two things immediately spring to mind: *lampredotto panini* (sandwiches of tender, abomasum tripe) and the colossal *bistecca alla fiorentina* (Florentine steak). The fact that these two dishes are meat dishes is no accident – Florentine cuisine is undeniably meat-heavy, with a preference for beef, pork and game.

As the Florentines have always been very good at not letting things go to waste, offal features heavily and heartily on the menu, in particular liver, tripe and the unique *lampredotto* (the fourth stomach of the cow). Florentines seem to be one of the only populations in the world to make good use of this ingredient, embracing it and making it their most beloved dish, *panini di lampredotto*. This delightfully rustic snack or breakfast is eaten warm while standing, usually on the street, next to the food van where it was made.

In comparison, there is relatively little fresh seafood on the Florentine menu. *Baccalà* (salted cod) makes an appearance here or there in dishes such as fried and battered cod or cooked in tomato sauce, but these dishes are better known in Rome or Livorno, respectively. It wasn't always this way, however, and some accounts dating to the 1300s describe abundant fresh fish available at the market, including fish from the city's own Arno river. However, the river was perhaps better used for other practical activities, such as washing away the foul-smelling activities of the centuries-old leather-tanning industry, performed on its banks; or diluting the unwanted muck from the Renaissance butchers' shops that once conveniently lined the Ponte Vecchio, the famous bridge whose picturesque shops are now brimming with gold and jewels.

'Florentine cuisine is undeniably meat-heavy, with a preference for beef, pork and game.'

Modern-day Florentine menus are more likely to feature game and, to a lesser extent, chicken than fresh fish. Chicken has historically been popular in Florence. During the Renaissance it was even considered medicinal and had restoring properties to help the sick and women who had just given birth. But it fell off menus drastically during the two world wars. After the Second World War, a whole chicken was considered quite an expensive meal, and most made do with cheaper cuts of meat – offal or the lesser cuts of beef that could be minced or stewed. Otherwise, dinner was something that could be hunted, such as wild boar, deer, rabbit, duck, pheasants or other birds. Game still has a strong presence on Florentine tables, taking pride of place in slow-cooked, hearty stews or dressing wide strips of fresh pappardelle noodles.

Many of the dishes in this chapter are arguably the stars of Florentine cuisine – the dishes that are constants on the city's restaurant and trattoria menus and indispensable on any Florentine table, particularly for a family gathering or celebration, such as *crostini di fegatini* (chicken liver crostini, page 183), *arista di maiale* (Florentine roast pork, page 199), *rosticciana* (grilled pork ribs, page 203) and the city's famous *bistecca alla fiorentina* (Florentine steak, page 186).

Others fall into the category of *cucina casalinga* (home cooking), ensuring nostalgia and comfort with every bite, from *braciole rifatte* (crumbed beef in tomato sauce, page 190) to *polpettone alla fiorentina* (Florentine meatloaf, page 200). And no Florentine menu would be complete without its offal – especially *trippa alla fiorentina* (Florentine-style tripe, page 196), delicious *polpette di trippa* (tripe meatballs, page 178) and wintry, oven-roasted *fegatelli di maiale* (pork liver parcels, page 192).

Crostini *di* Fegatini

CHICKEN LIVER PÂTÉ CROSTINI

1 baguette

1 medium onion, finely chopped

1 tablespoon extra-virgin olive oil

2 tablespoons butter

5 capers, rinsed and patted dry

2 anchovy fillets, drained of oil

500 g (1 lb 2 oz) chicken livers

100 ml (3½ fl oz) vin santo
   (or Marsala)

2–3 walnuts, optional

Also known as *crostini toscani* or *crostini neri* ('black crostini'), this dish is the definitive Tuscan antipasto. Rustic, tasty, cheap and sensible, these crostini are a constant on the menu of every trattoria in Florence, not to mention the kitchen tables at every special occasion, whether it's Easter, a birthday, Christmas or any family gathering in a Tuscan home.

Naturally, there are as many recipes for *crostini di fegatini* as there are cooks in Tuscany, with a few tweaks here and there. Usually, salted anchovies, capers or both are present – they provide that trademark Tuscan saltiness. Some like it smooth and some like it chunky, some go halfway. Red wine, stock or simply water can be used to cook the livers instead of the vin santo (the preference of Marco's nonna). And some like to add a few walnuts – a chef friend in Florence once told me it helps lend the pâté a nice, dark colour.

While these crostini are relatively simple in terms of presentation, for a classic Tuscan antipasto, serve these together with a platter of salumi, such as paper-thin slices of prosciutto and fennel seed-studded *finocchiona*, and wedges of pecorino cheese.

Preheat the oven to 140°C (275°F).

Slice the baguette into 1 cm (½ in) thick rounds and dry out in the oven for about 5 minutes before turning them over for another 5 minutes. The bread should be dry to the touch, but not browned. Set aside.

In a wide frying pan, cook the onion gently over low heat in olive oil and 1 tablespoon of the butter until soft and translucent, about 10 minutes. Add the capers and anchovies and continue to cook gently for a few minutes until the anchovies melt down.

Add the chicken livers and cook until browned on all sides, then add the vin santo and the walnuts, if using. Cook on low, uncovered, for about 30 minutes, adding water if necessary to keep the mixture moist. Season with salt and pepper and add the rest of the butter and let it melt.

Transfer the hot mixture to a food processor or blender and blend until mostly smooth (or all smooth, if you prefer).

Place heaped tablespoons of pâté onto the bread rounds and serve warm, if possible, or at room temperature. Alternatively, serve the warm pâté in a ceramic bowl with the bread rounds next to it and let guests help themselves.

MAKES ABOUT 20 CROSTINI

Pollo *al* Mattone

CHICKEN COOKED UNDER A BRICK

1 whole chicken, about 1 kg
  (2 lb 3 oz)
3 garlic cloves, sliced
10 fresh sage leaves, chopped
3 rosemary sprigs, leaves picked
  and chopped
2½ tablespoons extra-virgin olive oil
juice and zest of 1 lemon

NOTE
If you are using a slightly larger chicken, you may need to let it finish in the oven longer. A good test is to pierce the inside of the thigh with a skewer, if the juice runs clear, it is ready, if it is pink it still needs some more time.

This easy alternative to roast chicken supposedly dates to ancient Etruscan times. The marinated, butterflied chicken is cooked in an ovenproof frying pan under the weight of a brick (or try some heavy casserole dishes) to flatten it for even cooking and crisp skin. Chilli powder can also be added to the marinade, which makes this dish *pollo alla diavola*, named for the devilish heat of the spice. This chicken is also perfectly suited to cooking on a barbecue.

Butterfly the chicken by cutting along the backbone, removing it along with the wishbone and then flattening with the palm of your hand (alternatively, ask your butcher to do this). Disjoint the legs to flatten out further. Season the chicken generously inside and out with salt and pepper.

Make a marinade by combining the garlic, sage, rosemary, olive oil and lemon juice and zest. Rub this all over the chicken and under the skin and leave to marinate for at least 4 hours, or preferably overnight.

Preheat the oven to 180°C (360°F).

Prepare a clean brick by wrapping it in a double layer of aluminium foil. Remove the chicken from the marinade, (make sure to remove any garlic slices on the surface to avoid them burning). Rub the chicken with more olive oil.

Select an ovenproof frying pan that's large enough to hold the chicken. Sear the chicken over medium–high heat, skin side down, with the brick placed on top. Cook for 15 minutes. Carefully take off the brick (it will be hot), turn the chicken over, then replace the brick (using a side that wasn't previously touching the raw chicken) and cook the underside of the chicken for 15 minutes. Remove the brick, then finish cooking the chicken for a further 15 minutes.

Let the chicken rest for 10 minutes before serving.

SERVES 4

Pollo Fritto *alla* Fiorentina

FLORENTINE FRIED CHICKEN

1 kg (2 lb 3 oz) whole chicken,
    skin removed
1 rosemary sprig, coarsely chopped
1 bay leaf
1 garlic clove, sliced
juice of 1 lemon
1 litre (34 fl oz/4 cups) olive oil, plus
    extra for coating
125 g (4½ oz) plain (all-purpose)
    flour for dusting
2 eggs, beaten

This dish is often served as part of one great platter of *fritto misto*, along with mixed deep-fried vegetables, such as zucchini (courgette) flowers, tender artichoke quarters or fresh porcini mushrooms, depending on the season. In its simplest form, the marinade is forgone and the plain chicken pieces are simply dusted in flour and passed through beaten egg before being deep-fried.

Chop the chicken into eighteen pieces, four from the leg/thigh, two from the wings, and three from each breast. Place in a bowl with the rosemary, bay leaf, garlic, lemon juice and enough olive oil to coat the chicken – about 90 ml (3 fl oz). Marinate for at least 1 hour.

Remove the chicken from the marinade. Dust the chicken pieces with flour. Shake off the excess, then dip into the egg and place on a plate ready for deep- frying.

Preheat the oven to 140°C (275°F).

Heat the olive oil in a saucepan to 160°C (320°F). If you dont have a sugar thermometer, test the temperature by throwing in a little cube of bread. It should turn golden in about 20 seconds. Fry in two batches. After 5 minutes, turn the heat down to 140°C (275°F) and cook for 10 minutes, turning up the heat again for the last minute for a deep-brown colour. Drain on paper towel, place in a baking dish and keep warm in the oven, covered in foil, while you're frying the rest of the chicken.

Season the fried chicken with salt just before serving.

SERVES 4

Polpette *di* Trippa

TRIPE MEATBALLS

400 g (14 oz) boiled honeycomb
    tripe, about 500 g (1 lb 2 oz)
    if uncooked
80 g (2¾ oz) prosciutto (or pancetta
    or ham)
2 eggs
45 g (1½ oz/½ cup) grated pecorino
    or parmesan cheese
265 g (9½ oz) dry breadcrumbs
pinch of freshly ground nutmeg
1 handful flat-leaf parsley, chopped
100 g (3½ oz) plain (all-purpose)
    flour
olive oil for frying

Funnily enough, Artusi himself was not fond of tripe, saying, 'Tripe, however it is cooked and flavoured, is always ordinary.' Nevertheless, he suggests this recipe for deep-fried tripe meatballs to convert the indifferent or the squeamish – it's adapted from a cookbook dating to 1694. These meatballs make a delicious antipasto and are an easy way to get into using this cheap, nutritious, healthy ingredient.

In Florence, you can purchase already cooked tripe from the *trippaio* or *lampredottaio* (tripe or lampredotto vendors selling from food vans strategically dotted around the city), which saves time. If you buy it from your butcher, you will probably need to cook it (ask, just to be sure). To prepare tripe for this dish, simply place it in a stockpot of water with a whole, peeled onion and boil for 1 hour or until tender. You may need to add more water to keep the tripe sufficiently covered. When cooked, drain the tripe, rinse gently under running water and allow to cool before using in this recipe.

Finely mince the boiled tripe and prosciutto in a food processor. Add 1 egg, the cheese, 2 tablespoons of the breadcrumbs, the nutmeg, parsley and some salt and pepper. Continue blending until you have a well-combined, paste-like mixture.

Put three small bowls on the benchtop. Add the flour to one, beat the remaining egg in the other and add the remaining breadcrumbs to the third. Roll the tripe mixture into small balls about the size of a walnut, then dip each ball first into the flour, rolling to coat evenly, then in the beaten egg and finally into the breadcrumbs. Set aside until you have used up the mixture.

Heat enough olive oil in a small saucepan so that the balls will float. Heat the oil to about 180°C (360°F). If you don't have a sugar thermometer or similar to measure the temperature, throw a small cube of bread into the oil. At the right temperature, you should start to see little bubbles along the bottom of the pan. When the bread hits the oil it should immediately be surrounded by tiny little bubbles and turn nicely golden in about 15 seconds. At this point, turn the heat down a fraction and fry the balls until evenly deep golden brown and crisp. This should take about 1½ minutes. Carefully remove the tripe balls from the oil with a slotted spoon and drain on paper towel. Season with salt.

Serve hot as part of an antipasto, accompanied perhaps with some marinated olives or thinly sliced prosciutto.

MAKES ABOUT 20 MEATBALLS

Coniglio *con le* Olive

RABBIT & OLIVE STEW

600 g (1 lb 5 oz) rabbit

plain (all-purpose) flour for dusting

30–60 ml (1–2 fl oz) extra-virgin olive oil

1 onion, finely chopped

1 carrot, finely chopped

1 celery stalk, finely chopped

2 garlic cloves, chopped

1 rosemary sprig

5–10 fresh sage leaves

180 ml (6 fl oz) red wine

400 g (14 oz) tomato passata (puréed tomatoes) or tinned chopped tomatoes

1 litre (34 fl oz/4 cups) homemade vegetable stock or water

100 g (3½ oz) good quality black or green olives, such as taggiasche

1 handful flat-leaf parsley, chopped

A WORD OF WARNING

Be wary of the smaller bones floating around in the stew. If you're careful enough while chopping the rabbit, you can try to avoid using (or at least chopping through) the rib bones, which are the smallest, sharpest ones.

NOTE

If there are any leftovers, pick out the bones and simply toss the stew through some pappardelle pasta like you would a ragù. Even if there is no more meat left, but plenty of that delicious sauce, it still makes a wonderful pasta dish.

This traditional, countryside dish is also known as *coniglio alla cacciatora* (hunter's rabbit stew). The long, slow cooking, the briny olives and the resulting rich sauce help to create an extremely tasty, falling-off-the-bone stew – it's a wonderful way of cooking game meat. There are many ways to make this favourite Tuscan stew. In Florence, you'll find **cacciatora** in many guises and any game meat would be good cooked this way – pheasant, guinea fowl, venison or, even better, wild boar. If you can, use wild rabbit for a more traditional flavour – it is somewhat earthier and darker than farmed rabbit, which is more delicate. You could also use free-range chicken instead for a more delicate stew. This recipe is inspired by the way Marco's nonna Lina would have made it.

Prepare the rabbit by rinsing and patting dry with paper towel, removing the kidneys and liver if they are still intact, then chopping into pieces on the bone much like you would a chicken – hind legs (these can also be cut in half again), front legs, backstrap and tenderloin. You could also ask your butcher to do this for you.

Dust the pieces of rabbit with flour and shake off any excess. Pour the olive oil in a deep pan suitable for a stew, and sear the rabbit over medium–high heat until golden. Remove and set aside.

In the same pan, cook the onion, carrot and celery over a gentle heat until the onion becomes transparent and soft, about 10 minutes. Add the garlic and fresh herbs and continue cooking a few minutes until fragrant. Return the rabbit back to the pot, season with salt and pepper, add the wine and cook for a further couple of minutes.

Add the tomato to the pan with 2 cups of the stock (or water) and bring to a gentle simmer. Cook on the lowest heat until the meat begins to just fall off the bone, about 1½ hours (note that wild rabbit or other wild game may take a bit longer to become tender than farmed rabbit or chicken). If the sauce is getting too thick or dry, top up as needed with the stock or water (you may or may not need to use all of it).

Check the meat to see if it is tender. When it is ready, you can either remove the meat from the larger bones for easier eating or leave in large pieces.

In the meantime, remove the pits from the olives. Flatten them with the flat edge of a heavy knife and pull the pits out. Add the olives to the stew right at the end, along with the fresh parsley. Season with salt and pepper to taste.

Serve with roasted potatoes.

SERVES 4

Tagliata *di* Manzo
SEARED & SLICED STEAK

800 g (1 lb 12 oz) rump (sirloin)
or rib-eye (bone-in) steak, about
4 cm (1½ in) thick
1 rosemary sprig
125 ml (4 fl oz/½ cup) extra-virgin
olive oil
1 handful rocket (arugula), to serve
shaved parmesan, to serve

This is a very simple preparation, a favourite on the menus of trattorie or restaurants when a *bistecca fiorentina* is a bit too much but customers still crave a good steak. Like the *bistecca*, this is always cooked rare or, at the most, medium–rare in Florence. Served with a scattering of fresh rocket (arugula) and shaved parmesan, this dish is a meal on its own. Don't forget some good crusty bread to mop up the juices.

Remove the meat from the refrigerator 1 hour before cooking to bring it up to room temperature.

Bash the rosemary with the palm of your hand on the chopping board to release the essential oil, and drop in the olive oil in a small jug or bowl and let infuse for 1 hour.

Heat a chargrill pan to maximum heat. Season the meat with salt and brush over some of the rosemary-infused oil. When the pan begins to smoke, turn down the heat just a little and immediately place the steak in the pan.

Cook for 4 minutes on each side, turning every 2 minutes, then cook for a further 2 minutes on the bone side, holding the steak upright with a pair of tongs. Transfer the meat to a plate, pour over the rest of the rosemary-infused oil and cover with aluminium foil to rest for 4–6 minutes.

Slice the meat into 1.5 cm (½ in) thick pieces, season with freshly ground pepper and salt flakes and serve topped with fresh rocket, shaved parmesan and the oily juices left over from resting the meat.

SERVES 4

Bistecca *alla* Fiorentina

FLORENTINE STEAK

2 T-bone steaks, weighing about 1 kg
    (2 lb 3 oz) each, 4 cm (1½ in) thick
extra-virgin olive oil (optional)

Bistecca, the enormous Florentine steak, impresses because of its size but is humbly and simply dressed in just salt and pepper, relying on the flavour and texture of particularly lean Tuscan beef to make it the hero of this city's cuisine. I think it is best described by Aldo Santini, Tuscan gastronome and writer, who calls *bistecca* 'the Giotto' of the food world, referring to the medieval Florentine master who is considered the grandfather of the Renaissance.

Taking its name from the English word 'beefsteak', the preparation of *bistecca* supposedly dates back to at least the 1500s and there is a popular legend of grilled steaks being prepared for the Florentines by the Medici family in honour of the saint day of San Lorenzo, August 10, in the piazza of the church dedicated to the saint. Incidentally, San Lorenzo (Saint Lawrence) is also the patron saint of cooks. Grilled to death, during his execution he is reported to have said, 'I'm done on this side, now turn me over and eat me!' and is often depicted carrying his trademark grill. I can't help but think that the steak grilling and the saint's martyrdom are morbidly connected.

Tradition states that *bistecca alla fiorentina* should come from Chianina cattle, an ancient Tuscan breed and one of the world's largest – mature bulls reach over 1.8 metres (nearly 6 feet) tall. These huge, white creatures were long used as working animals for their size and strength, but more recently they have become prized for their meat. While tasty, the beef is very lean and therefore has a tendency to become tough when cooked.

In a restaurant, *bistecca alla fiorentina* is always priced by weight and is usually the most expensive item on the menu, for good reason. It's a sizeable steak and it is normally meant for at least two diners. A good trattoria or restaurant will cut the steak to order, based on the number of servings, and they will show you the steak before they cook it. A portion can be around 600–800 g (1 lb 5 oz–1 lb 12 oz), including the bone, so it's not unusual to see the waiter bring out a hunk of meat weighing over a kilogram when it's meant to be shared between two.

Bistecca is best eaten with the usual side dishes, such as crisp, roasted rosemary potatoes, sautéed greens or cannellini beans 'all'olio' (page 101) and, naturally, plenty of Tuscan bread to mop up the precious juices.

Remove the meat from the refrigerator 1 hour before cooking to bring it to room temperature. Do not season before cooking.

The bistecca is traditionally cooked over hot coals in a fireplace. A barbecue works well too, but a chargrill pan or a heavy-duty cast-iron frying pan on the stove top will suffice. For this quantity, you may need to cook one steak at a time. Keep one warm, covered with aluminium foil, until the other steak is ready.

Set a frying pan over high heat. When hot, add the steak and cook for 3–5 minutes – less time if it is 3.5 cm (1½ in) thick, more if it is 5 cm (2 in) thick. Turn once and cook the other side the same amount of time. Then turn the steak onto the bone side (like an upside-down T) – hold it upright with tongs – and cook for 2–3 minutes.

Remove from the heat and season with salt flakes and pepper. Let it rest, meat still on the bone if possible, for 10 minutes, covered in foil. The meat should be well browned outside, rare inside, and the fat should be glistening and transparent.

Cut the steak around the bone, then into thick slices – about 1.5–2 cm (½–¾ in) thick. Serve the meat recomposed with the T-bone (some enjoy gnawing on this), with a scant drizzle of very good extra-virgin olive oil, if desired.

SERVES 4

'For those who like their meat well done, there are two options: either be adventurous and try this as it should be eaten, or eat something else.'

The Art of Bistecca

There is an art to cooking, ordering and eating *bistecca alla fiorentina*.

First, it must be rare. Not just blushing, but bloody. As a lean meat, it is most tender this way, and even then, part of the pleasure in eating this steak is that it should be chewed slowly and pensively. It's rather primal, but it's as if with each bite you get more flavour out of it. For those who like their meat well done, there are two options: either be adventurous and try this as it should be eaten, or eat something else. A number of Florentine trattorie have cheekily resorted to attaching signs to their menus announcing to the tourists who request well-done *bistecca* that the kitchen will not do it and to respect tradition! In any case, over-cooking dishonours this beautiful, very lean meat, which would only get ruined by disagreeable leatheriness and toughness the longer it cooks. Most agree with Artusi, who says 'the beauty' of the steak's rareness is that when you cut into it, out pours the most wonderful 'sauce' of its own.

The bistecca must be on the bone (a T-bone), with the tender fillet that makes up about a third of the steak attached and the entire thing about 'two fingers' thick – depending on the fingers: about 3.5–4 cm (1½ in) thick, at the very most 5 cm (2 in). The thickness of a good *bistecca* seems to have changed over the decades. Pellegrino Artusi (1891) advises 1 to 1½ fingers thick; Ada Boni in *The Talisman* (1929) says 2.5 cm (1 in).

The final rule is no sauce. The only thing this steak needs is some salt, *after* it has come off the grill, some freshly ground black pepper and perhaps a drizzle of extra-virgin olive oil. But I recall a retired butcher once telling me that a real *bistecca alla fiorentina* doesn't even need salt. It is tasty enough as it is, he claimed.

Braciole Rifatte

CRUMBED BEEF IN TOMATO SAUCE

4 thin slices of lean veal or beef,
about 100 g (3½ oz) per slice
1 egg, beaten
65 g (2¼ oz/⅔ cup) dry breadcrumbs
90 ml (3 fl oz) extra-virgin olive oil
1 garlic clove, finely chopped
400 g (14 oz) tinned tomatoes,
chopped or peeled
250 ml (8½ fl oz/1 cup) homemade
beef stock or water
2–3 flat-leaf parsley sprigs,
finely chopped
Tuscan bread (or other crusty bread),
to serve

This classic Florentine dish is one of many with the title '*rifatte*', meaning 'redone', a great example of how thrifty Florentines know how to give a second life to leftovers by recooking them with tomatoes. Naturally, this is a dish that changes from household to household and largely depends on what you already have on hand. This particular recipe is inspired by one from Trattoria Mario (see page 243), one of the city's best and most traditional trattorie.

This is a truly economical main dish – the reason it has always been popular in home cooking as well as old-school canteens – and the cheaper ingredients are actually its best feature. Begin with very thin slices – pound them with a meat mallet if you like to make them even flatter and wider – and a heaping amount of breadcrumbs which will soak up the sauce and plump up the *braciole* like sponges. And serve with plenty of sauce and a basket of sliced Tuscan bread. The bread here – both in the breadcrumb mixture and in the obligatory *scarpetta* (when you sop up the leftover sauce on your plate with sliced bread) – is what actually fills up hungry diners, enabling the clever cook to satisfy many with a relatively small amount of meat.

Pound the meat with a mallet if desired, to make the slices very flat and wide. Put the beaten egg and the breadcrumbs in two separate shallow bowls. Dip the meat first in the egg, then coat in the breadcrumbs, pressing down well and ensuring they are well covered.

Pour about 60 ml (2 fl oz/¼ cup) of olive oil into a wide frying pan over medium heat. Fry meat on both sides until golden brown and crisp. The timing will depend on your preferred thickness of meat. Set aside to drain on paper towel.

Prepare the tomato sauce. In the same pan you used to fry the meat, heat the rest of the olive oil over low–medium heat and gently cook the garlic until soft and slightly golden. Add the tomatoes, breaking them up with your spoon, and stock (or water), then season with salt and pepper. Simmer, uncovered, for 10 minutes.

Add the cooked meat to the tomato sauce, making sure they are completely submerged in the tomato sauce. Allow to simmer over a medium heat until the meat becomes swollen with the sauce and the sauce thickens. If it begins to get dry, add more stock (or water) as necessary.

Serve the braciole with plenty of sauce, parsley scattered over the top and crusty bread to wipe your plate clean.

SERVES 4

Fegatelli *di* Maiale

PORK LIVER PARCELS

250 g (9 oz) caul fat

1 tablespoon vinegar

500 g (1 lb 2 oz) pork liver, cut into
4 cm (1½ in) pieces

2 tablespoons dry breadcrumbs

2 teaspoons dried fennel seeds,
crushed

fresh bay leaves

wild fennel seed heads, stalks
attached (or bay leaf stalks, leaves
removed, or toothpicks)

250 g (9 oz) lard *or* olive oil to cover
(see notes below)

NOTES

Fresh bay leaves are important for
this dish. If you can't find them, do
not substitute with dried bay leaves –
use fresh sage instead.

Cooking in lard is the most traditional
method, but you could also use olive
oil in the same way, including heating
it in the oven for the first 20 minutes
before adding the fegatelli. This
technique of slow cooking in fat – and
you can use any fat for this – is known
as confit. It is also traditional to use
the stalks of the dried fennel seed
heads or bay leaves (minus the leaves)
to pierce the fegatelli, but a toothpick
can also be used. They are usually left
long and poking out upright from the
dish so that it is easy to pick up the
fegatelli without burning fingers.

There is no substitute for caul fat
(it is truly vital to the dish in terms of
appearance, flavour and method). It's
used to keep the liver moist as it cooks
and melts down to create a delicious
crust. Ask for it at the butcher, or you
may find it more easily frozen. Either
way, it should be soaked in water and
vinegar before using (the frozen one
should be thawed first).

This is a dish close to my heart as it is my husband Marco's favourite meal.
It reminds him of home, especially of his father, who also loved this dish.
It is comfort food, nostalgic food, at its best.

An ancient and seasonal meal that is mentioned in cookbooks as far
back as the fourteenth century, this dish is usually made in winter (and
therefore commonly prepared for Christmas or New Year's Eve, like my
in-laws do) when pigs are traditionally slaughtered and fresh pork liver
is available. There are a number of different ways *fegatelli* are prepared,
depending on how far you stray from Florence. Each town has their own
recipe, though they are all variations on the same theme. Towards Siena,
the liver is minced rather than left in whole pieces and sometimes mixed
with sausage mince. Sometimes the earthy little parcels of pork liver,
wrapped in the lacy bodice-like encasing of caul fat, are threaded onto
long skewers with alternating pieces of pork, bay leaves and slices of bread
and baked with a dousing of white wine.

The lard in which the *fegatelli* are cooked has always been a traditional
way of conserving food before the advent of refrigeration. When cool, the
lard hardens, creating an air-proof environment that keeps the cooked
fegatelli fresh for about a month at room temperature. When ready to eat,
you just need to reheat and melt the lard to free the *fegatelli*. I love the
way the fennel seed stalks become very useful here, not just for flavouring,
but for fishing the *fegatelli* out of bubbling hot lard.

This is the way Marco loves his *fegatelli*: golf-ball-sized whole chunks
of liver, flavoured with the obligatory bay leaf and crushed wild fennel
seeds – the scent and flavour of fennel is one of the strongest and most
characteristic aromas of Tuscan cooking for me. They are dressed in a
cloak of caul fat and roasted until blushing pink inside.

It is important not to overcook these, as they become tough and chewy
to the point of inedible. Andrea, a butcher friend from Fucecchio's
neighbour, San Miniato (where you will find his family's excellent shop,
Sergio Falaschi Macelleria – a must if you are in the area), suggested this
slow-roasting technique here to avoid over-cooking. If your oven is not
reliable at such a low temperature, you can also cook these on the stove
top by melting the lard in a small pot (traditionally a terracotta one is
used) and then submerging the *fegatelli* in one layer in the bubbling, hot
lard. Cook over low heat for about 30 minutes or until golden brown.

Recipe continued overleaf ›

If you're not planning to serve the fegatelli straight away, after removing them from the oven, let them cool in the baking dish (making sure they are fully submerged in the lard) until the lard solidifies. They will keep very well like this in the refrigerator for months. To serve, warm up the lard in a low oven until melted then remove the fegatelli and brown them, as described in the recipe.

Rinse the caul fat in a bowl of cold water with vinegar. Drain, lay it flat on a chopping board and roughly cut into squares large enough to wrap around and cover each piece of liver – about 10 cm (4 in).

Combine the breadcrumbs, fennel seed, and some salt and pepper.

Preheat the oven to 80°C (180°F).

In the centre of each square of caul fat, place a bay leaf. Roll each piece of liver in the breadcrumb mixture to coat, then place onto the bay leaf, wrapping the fat tightly around the liver. Trim any excess with a sharp knife and hold the 'package' together by piercing with the wild fennel stalk (a bay leaf stalk or toothpick can substitute).

Place the lard in a baking dish that will fit all the fegatelli in one layer. Place in the oven for 20 minutes. Submerge the fegatelli in the lard and return to the oven for another 20–25 minutes. The caul fat should melt and become transparent, and the fegatelli should be blushing pink inside but not bloody. Brown them in a pan over medium heat, rolling or turning them occasionally until evenly crisp and golden brown, a few minutes.

These go well with sautéed Tuscan kale, silverbeet (Swiss chard) or other greens, tossed with some garlic and olive oil.

SERVES 4

Trippa *alla* Fiorentina

FLORENTINE-STYLE TRIPE

800 g (1 lb 12 oz) honeycomb tripe
1 onion, finely chopped
5–6 flat-leaf parsley stalks, finely
    chopped (reserve the leaves for
    garnish, if desired)
3 tablespoons extra-virgin olive oil
250 ml (8½ fl oz/1 cup) white wine
2 tablespoons tomato paste
    (concentrated purée)
400 g (14 oz) tomato passata
    (puréed tomatoes)
1 handful fresh marjoram leaves
    (or oregano)
Tuscan bread (or other crusty bread),
    to serve
finely grated parmesan cheese,
    to serve

Made at home as often as it is eaten out at a favourite trattoria, this recipe is inspired by my husband's aunt, Franca, who is not only a lover of offal but also indisputably the best cook in the family. She casually gave me this recipe one day while we were standing on the street, recounting (in the way that happens when you share a recipe orally) the order of ingredients but not the amounts, and the way it should look but not the cooking times. So I have reconstructed it, changing one important thing: in her tomato sauce, she uses solely tomato paste (concentrated purée), which she explains makes it more flavourful. Tripe is delicate in flavour, almost sweet, so the more intense paste helps to give it some oomph. I like it with a bit more tomato to it so I have added tomato passata (puréed tomatoes) to achieve a happy medium. It goes without saying that this dish is even better the next day, when the flavours have settled.

Slice the tripe thinly into strips – about 5 cm (2 in) long and no more than 1 cm (½ in) thick. Rinse the tripe under running water or even blanch momentarily in boiling water.

Cook the onion and parsley stalks in a large saucepan or stockpot in the olive oil over a gentle heat. When the onion is soft and translucent, add the tripe and cook, stirring, for a further 5 minutes. Add the wine, turn the heat up to medium and cook for a further 10 minutes.

Add the tomato paste and passata and turn the heat down to low–medium. Cook for a further 20–30 minutes, uncovered, stirring occasionally. The tripe should be tender but still al dente, like pasta. Season with salt and pepper to taste and add the marjoram leaves (and reserved parsley leaves, if desired).

Serve in shallow bowls with a generous sprinkling of parmesan cheese, and crusty bread for dipping.

SERVES 4

Arista *di* Maiale

FLORENTINE PORK ROAST

1 kg (2 lb 3 oz) bone-in pork
  loin or rib roast
extra-virgin olive oil, for rubbing
1 rosemary sprig, leaves picked and
  finely chopped
8–10 sage leaves, finely chopped
2 garlic cloves
125 ml (4 fl oz/½ cup) white wine

This roast pork has been a fixture of Florentine cooking since at least the Renaissance, or so the legend goes. Artusi traces the origins of its unusual name to 1439 when, during an international assembly of bishops in Florence, this roast was served. It was received with such enthusiasm that a guest exclaimed, 'Àrista, arista', meaning 'the best'.

Nothing is wasted in a Florentine kitchen. The pan drippings that result from making *arista* are liquid gold. Peel and chop some potatoes to add to the bottom of the pan where they will catch all the drippings – they will be the best roast potatoes you'll ever have. Or toss some blanched cavolo nero (black Tuscan kale) or cooked cannellini (lima) beans (page 101) through the pan juices, after removing the *arista* from the oven and while it is resting. This is enough for four but you'll hopefully get some leftovers out of this – it's even better cold the next day, in thin slices.

The pork needs to be at room temperature before cooking. If taking the pork out of the refrigerator, cover it in plastic wrap, and allow it to sit for at least 1 hour. Cut all along the bone, as if you were removing the bone completely, but leave it attached by about 3 cm (1¼ in) at the bottom. Rub olive oil all over the meat.

Preheat the oven to 160°C (320°F).

Mix the rosemary leaves, sage and garlic, and add some salt and pepper. Place half of this herb mix along the cut just made and with the rest, rub it in and around the rest of the meat. Tie with string to hold the roast together and cover the bones with aluminium foil to keep them from burning.

Place the roast, skin side up, on a metal cooling rack in a baking pan so it is not touching the bottom of the pan. Pour the white wine over the roast so that it coats the meat and drips into the tray. Bake for about 50 minutes. If you have a meat thermometer, you are looking for an interior temperature of about 65°C (150°F).

Remove from the oven, turn the heat to 220°C (430°F) and place back in the oven for a further 5 minutes to crisp up the skin. Rest the meat for at least 15 minutes, uncovered, then slice thickly using the bones as guides and serve.

SERVES 4

Polpettone *alla* Fiorentina

FLORENTINE MEATLOAF

400 g (14 oz) lean minced (ground) beef

100 g (3½ oz) prosciutto, finely chopped

40 g (1½ oz) pecorino or parmesan cheese, grated

1 egg

pinch of nutmeg

pinch of ground fennel seeds

plain (all-purpose) flour for dusting

2 tablespoons extra-virgin olive oil

½ celery stalk, finely chopped

1 small carrot, finely chopped

1 onion, finely chopped

a pinch of salt

400 g (14 oz) tomato passata (puréed tomatoes)

2 fresh bay leaves

1 rosemary sprig

Tuscan bread (or other crusty bread) to serve

NOTE

If you can make the meatloaf in advance or have leftovers, the meatloaf can be sliced when cool, which is easier. It can then be reheated gently and very carefully in the sauce, and it will be all the tastier the next day as well.

Meatloaf is not the prettiest dish but it is homely and incredibly satisfying, a meal that will feed the whole family and hopefully give you some leftovers, too. In fact, like so many Florentine dishes, this is better the day after it is cooked. Those in the know actually wait until the next day to serve it, because when it's sliced cool it tends to crumble less. Some like to brush egg white over the loaf to help hold it together.

Serve *polpettone* in thick slices with a generous dollop of tomato sauce heaped over the top, some crusty Tuscan bread and a green salad or some spinach sautéed with some garlic and olive oil.

In a wide bowl, combine the beef, prosciutto, cheese, egg, nutmeg, fennel seeds and season generously with salt and pepper. Shape into a compact loaf, patting down firmly, then place on a plate or tray, covered in plastic wrap, and chill in the refrigerator for at least 30 minutes.

Dust the meatloaf evenly in a light coating of flour. Heat the olive oil in a stockpot over medium heat and sear the meatloaf to brown on all sides, turning carefully. With the meatloaf still in the pan, turn the heat down to low and add the celery, carrot, onion and salt. Cook gently, stirring around the meatloaf so as not to disturb it, until the vegetables are soft, about 10 minutes.

Add the tomato passata, 200 ml (7 fl oz) water and the herbs, and season again with salt and pepper. Let it simmer, covered, for 50 minutes. Remove the lid and continue cooking until the sauce has thickened slightly, at least 10 more minutes. Remove the bay leaves and rosemary sprig before serving.

Cut the meatloaf into slices about 2 cm (¾ in) thick. Serve a slice of meatloaf with a generous dollop of the sauce over the top and with crusty bread.

SERVES 4

Rosticciana

GRILLED PORK RIBS

1 kg (2 lb 3 oz) pork ribs
1 teaspoon salt
60 ml (2 fl oz/¼ cup) extra-virgin
   olive oil
1 rosemary sprig
2 garlic cloves, thinly sliced

This is one of those dishes that you would order in a trattoria or have at a gathering at home when there are plenty of people to share it with. In a trattoria, *grigliata mista* (literally 'mixed grill') is a wonderful, large metal platter of *rosticciana*, salty and stout fennel-studded Tuscan sausages, grilled chicken and perhaps some pork on skewers or rare grilled steak. These ribs go well with traditional side dishes such as roast potatoes, stewed cannellini beans 'all'olio' (page 101) or green beans dressed in tomato sauce (page 110). A simple green salad works, too.

Season the ribs with ½ teaspoon of the salt, some freshly ground pepper and a drizzle of the olive oil.

Grill over a preheated barbecue (charcoal, preferably) for 30 minutes, turning every 3–4 minutes. Use the rosemary sprig to brush the rest of the olive oil over the ribs at every turn. If the barbecue gets too hot, remove the meat from the hot spot or remove completely until the fire cools a little.

Test whether the ribs are adequately cooked by poking the meat with the tip of a sharp knife. If it meets no resistance, they're ready.

Prepare a dressing with the remaining olive oil and salt, some pepper and the garlic. When the ribs are cooked, place them on a serving plate and coat with the dressing. Serve immediately – there is no other way but to eat with your hands.

SERVES 4

Peposo

BEEF & PEPPER STEW

2 tablespoons extra-virgin olive oil
1 kg (2 lb 3 oz) good stewing or
  braising beef, such as chuck, diced
3 garlic cloves, whole but peeled
750 ml (25½ fl oz/3 cups) red wine,
  preferably Chianti
a good pinch of salt
1 tablespoon freshly ground black
  pepper
Tuscan bread (or other crusty bread),
  to serve

This historic dish hails from the little town of Impruneta, 15 kilometres (about 9 miles) outside Florence. Known for its terracotta, it's the town where Renaissance architect Filippo Brunelleschi sourced the brown-red tiles of the dome of Florence's Duomo in the 1400s. It is said that Brunelleschi often lunched on a bowl of this hearty beef stew, slowly cooked at the mouth of the same ovens that baked the terracotta itself.

There are plenty of modern versions of this dish that include herbs or root vegetables and, commonly, tomato paste (concentrated purée) or passata (puréed tomatoes), but the classic, essential version of this dish is so wonderful in its simplicity that it really doesn't need anything other than a whole bottle of Chianti and a good dose of garlic and black pepper. Don't be alarmed by the amount of pepper called for in this dish – it's not called *peposo* ('peppery') for nothing.

Heat the olive oil in a heavy-based stockpot. Brown the meat in batches over medium heat, then return all the meat back to the pot and add the garlic, red wine, salt and pepper. Simmer, covered, for 2½ hours, or until the meat is very tender but not falling apart. Remove the lid of the pot for the last 45 minutes to reduce the liquid to a thick sauce.

Serve with plenty of Tuscan bread to mop up the sauce.

SERVES 4

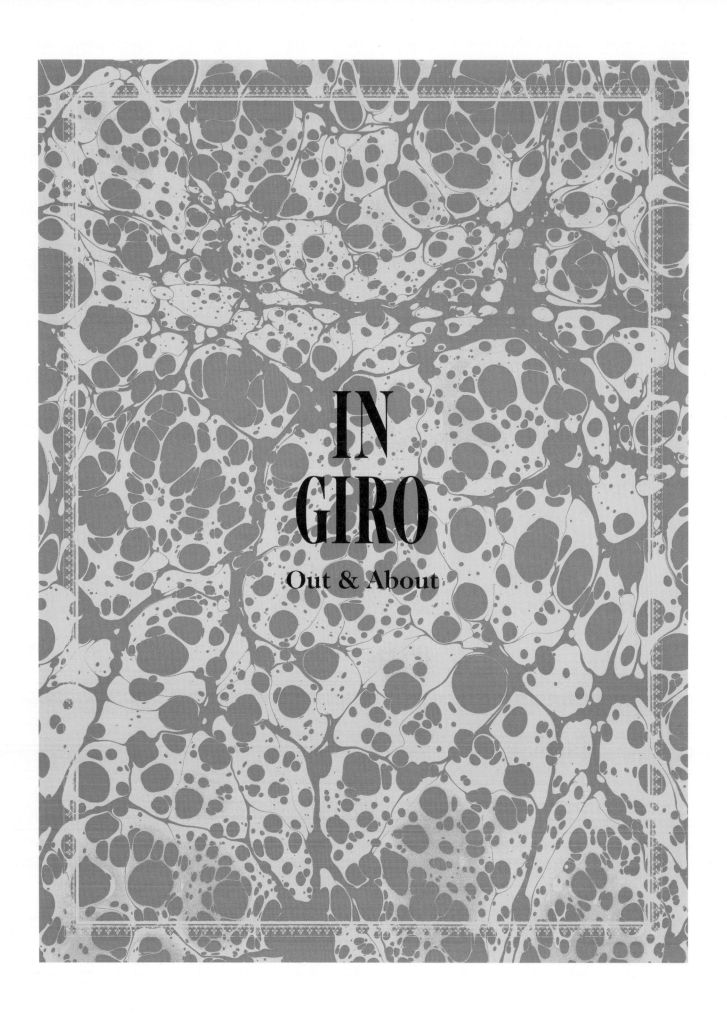

IN GIRO

Out & About

Crostini *con* Lardo, Miele *e* Pepe
CROSTINI WITH LARDO, HONEY & PEPPER

Crostini *con* Pecorino, Pera *e* Noci
CROSTINI WITH PECORINO, PEAR & WALNUTS

Crostini *con* Burro *e* Acciughe
CROSTINI WITH BUTTER & ANCHOVIES

Crostone *con* Salsiccia *e* Stracchino
CROSTONE WITH SAUSAGE & STRACCHINO CHEESE

Panini Tartufati
TRUFFLE SANDWICHES

Panino *con* Finocchiona, Melanzane *e* Stracchino
PANINO WITH FINOCCHIONA, EGGPLANT & STRACCHINO CHEESE

Panino *con* Spinaci *e* Brie
WARM BRIE & SPINACH ROLL

Panino *con* Lampredotto *e* Salsa Verde
LAMPREDOTTO PANINO WITH SALSA VERDE

Panino *col* Peposo
PANINO BOWL WITH BEEF STEW

Panino *con* Insalata Belga, Pecorino *e* Miele
PANINO WITH WITLOF, PECORINO & HONEY

Gelato *di* Riso
RICE GELATO

Gelato *al* Fior *di* Latte
MILK GELATO

Sorbetto *di* Susine
PLUM SORBET

'The *enoteca* is where you'll get the best selection of good, wine-friendly *stuzzichini* – snacks such as crostini, that will 'open your stomach', as the Florentines like to say, but not ruin your appetite for dinner.'

Florence has always had a great street food scene and an excellent selection of hole-in-the-wall places that offer a quick and tasty bite to eat, made on the spot. Freshly made panini, prepared with quick hands and quality produce (including local cheeses and salumi sliced to order), are a specialty of the winding streets of Florence's historic centre. Without a doubt, *lampredotto panini* are the culinary symbol of the city – and a tradition that dates back to the Renaissance. Nowhere else in the world can you find anything like these warm rolls filled with boiled beef offal and lashings of salsa verde. Typically sold from a van before food vans became the popular thing, these panini can be found in strategic points all around the city.

In the evening, after work, the locals stop by their favourite *enoteca* (wine bar) to meet friends for a glass of wine before heading home or out to dinner. The tradition of an *aperitivo* (aperitif) at this golden hour is one that is found in all types of bars, but undoubtedly the *enoteca* is where you'll get the best selection of good, wine-friendly *stuzzichini* (bites to eat) – snacks such as crostini, that will 'open your stomach', as the Florentines like to say, but not ruin your appetite for dinner.

A good meal out is commonly rounded off with a *passeggiata* (stroll), partially to walk off dinner but also to reach the nearest artisan gelateria for a smooth gelato, whipped out of metal tubs with a spatula into little cups. This is a favourite pastime in summer, especially when gelaterie remain open until midnight.

When out and about in Florence, you may come across some of the places that have inspired this chapter's recipes, an easy way to bring a bit of the city's street food culture into your home. There are those little spots to sit and enjoy a glass of wine along with some crostini with an array of flavourful toppings, such as the classic combination of creamy butter and anchovies or a balance of sweet and salty with lardo, honey and pepper and little truffled sandwiches for something a bit special. Or you may stumble across some of the city's best *paninoteche* (panino joints), where you can grab a quick and cheap lunch filled with simple but delicious combinations, from warm brie and spinach rolls to the famous *lampredotto panini*. And don't forget the gelateria – here I've included three of my favourite gelato flavours.

Wine Doors

Dotted throughout Florence, usually nestled into the side wall of a noble Renaissance palazzo, a unique Florentine curiosity can be found: a small doorway with a stone arch that often mimics the palazzo's main entrance. These miniature doors – positioned at chest level and just tall enough to fit a flask of wine through – are known as *buchette del vino* (literally 'wine holes'). Dating back to a period of decline in the seventeenth century, these little doors allowed wine to be bought and sold discreetly to passers-by on the street, allowing the struggling aristocratic families to make a little money on the side from the wine produced from their own vineyards.

A wonderful example is the well-preserved buchetta on the wall of Palazzo Antinori, next to the restaurant Buca Lapi on via del Trebbio, a palazzo that still belongs to the family bearing one of the city's biggest names in winemaking. The word 'vino' etched into the stone archway of the walled-in buchetta is really the only reminder of the long-forgotten function of the buchette del vino. In their place are today's hole-in-the-wall wine bars, which, like everything in Florentine culture, are born out of tradition and steeped in the city's history.

Crostini *con* Lardo, Miele *e* Pepe

CROSTINI WITH LARDO, HONEY & PEPPER

4 slices of baguette, about 1 cm
    (½ in) thick
120 g (4½ oz) asiago or young
    pecorino cheese, thinly sliced
16 very thin slices of lardo, about
    60 g (2 oz)
1 teaspoon runny honey
freshly ground black pepper

NOTE

Ask at your local gourmet deli about
the availability of lardo. Note that the
next best substitute is pancetta, sliced
paper-thin so that it's not too salty.

One of my favourite pastimes on a particularly cool, wet evening is to
warm up with a glass of wine at Le Volpi e l'Uva, a wine bar tucked away
in a little piazza next to the church of Santa Felicità. One of the real
enoteche of Florence, this place focuses on wine. There's no kitchen, just
a small counter where little plates of small-producer, artisan-made salumi
and cheese and a few very good crostini – like this one – are prepared to
whet appetites.

Lardo is a beautiful product – it is not lard, as many mistakenly think, but
carefully cured back fat, full of flavour, with a silky, melting texture. This
is a delicious combination that cleverly pairs the saltiness of lardo with the
sweetness of honey.

Toast the bread under a grill (broiler) or in the oven lightly to dry it out and give
it some crunch.

Place the cheese on the warm bread and place under a grill briefly or until the
cheese has melted. Top with the lardo in overlapping layers – the warmth of the
melted cheese and hot bread should make the lardo warm and soften and become
ever so slightly transparent around the edges. Drizzle over the honey and grind
over some pepper.

MAKES 4 CROSTINI

Crostini *con* Pecorino, Pera e Noci

CROSTINI WITH PECORINO, PEAR & WALNUTS

4 slices of baguette, about 1 cm
  (½ in) thick
8 walnut halves
60 g (2 oz) pecorino cheese, sliced
1 large pear, peeled, cored and
  thinly sliced
2 teaspoons runny honey

This is a popular combination of ingredients that I have seen done in countless ways across Florence, from ravioli to gelato – and for good reason, too. Eating these particular crostini always reminds me of the wonderful spread of crostini on offer at Enoteca Fuori Porta, a little wine bar–restaurant that is, as its name suggests, just outside the gate of the old city wall. You can try this with a softer style of cheese (such as brie or even gorgonzola) in place of the pecorino.

Preheat the oven to 180°C (360°F).

Toast the bread under a grill (broiler) or in the oven lightly to dry it out and give it some crunch.

Line a baking tray with baking paper and place the walnuts in a single layer on top. Toast in the oven for 5–10 minutes, or until you can begin to smell a toasted aroma. Watch that they do not burn, as they will become bitter. Remove from the oven and roughly chop.

Top the toasted bread with the pecorino cheese and a couple of slices of pear and place under the grill to melt the cheese.

Serve warm, topped with walnuts, freshly ground pepper, and a drizzle of honey.

MAKES 4 CROSTINI

Crostini Burro e Acciughe

CROSTINI WITH BUTTER & ANCHOVIES

2 slices of country bread, cut into
two, *or* 4 slices of baguette about
1 cm (½ in) thick
20 g (¾ oz) unsalted butter, at room
temperature
4 anchovy fillets, rinsed or drained

NOTE

To get closer to the real thing, try
an unsalted, cultured (also known
as European-style) butter, which
you may be able to find produced
locally as well as imported. The more
complex flavour and rich mouthfeel
of this style of butter will mean a
world of difference in this simple but
very satisfying recipe.

In Florence, crostoni and crostini make popular snacks, whether for
antipasto or aperitivo (depending on what time of day it is). Think of them
as an open-faced toastie, usually grilled or served warm but not always.
Most may immediately think of the famous bruschetta, a crostone of
toasted, garlic-rubbed bread topped with tomato, olive oil and basil.

The difference between crostoni and crostini all comes down to size. The
–one suffix in *crostone* (*crostoni* when plural) implies that it's a big one,
usually made with a wide slice of Tuscan bread. A *crostino* (*crostini* when
plural), with its *–ino* suffix, is small, and made with baguette rounds or
Tuscan bread cut into smaller pieces – you could finish one in about two
bites. A large crostone might serve as a hearty snack or even lunch, or part
of an aperitivo or antipasto if shared. Crostini make good starters and are
almost always part of an antipasto platter, perhaps with a mix of toppings
which almost always includes chicken liver pâté, amongst others such as
this one.

These crostini balance the sweet creaminess of quality, unsalted butter
with a salty kick from the anchovy, which makes this classic (and thrifty)
combination such a good one. If you can, try to get anchovies conserved
in salt rather than the ones in oil for this – the extra flavour is worth it.
Salted anchovies just need to be thoroughly rinsed of salt in cold water
(even soaked, some say, and do for at least 10 minutes) and then sliced
in half lengthways and their spines removed – it pulls out easily – before
using. Each salted anchovy gives you two fillets. If using regular anchovy
fillets in oil, pull them out of the jar with a fork and drain each fillet
thoroughly on paper towels before using.

Toast the bread under a grill (broiler) or in the oven lightly to dry it out and give
it some crunch.

When cool, spread the butter over the crostini and top with an anchovy.

MAKES 4 CROSTINI

Crostone *con* Salsiccia *e* Stracchino

CROSTONE WITH SAUSAGE & STRACCHINO CHEESE

4 slices of Tuscan bread, 1 cm
   (½ in) thick (or use a similar
   large crusty loaf)
200 g (7 oz) good-quality pork
   sausages
120 g (4½ oz) stracchino cheese
   (or other good melting cheese)
a pinch of salt
splash of balsamic vinegar

NOTE

Stracchino cheese can be hard to
find outside Italy unless you have an
artisan Italian cheese maker nearby,
as it is so fresh and is best eaten the
day it's made. Some good alternatives
are fresh (and deliciously gooey)
squacquerone or a good, mild melting
cheese like asiago, which should be
grated into the sausage meat.

I always order the sausage crostone when I visit my favourite wine bar, Le Volpi e l'Uva. They make this with truffled sausages, which are pretty special. The next best thing to use is good quality pork and fennel sausages. You could really use any good melting cheese for this, but *stracchino* – a very fresh, gooey, spreadable cheese – is the best partner.

The idea of adding the balsamic vinegar comes from another little wine bar in Florence, Casa del Vino, which arguably makes the best panini in town. Tuscans will eat this sausage and cheese filling raw, but in this recipe, the crostone is grilled.

Toast the bread under a grill (broiler) or in the oven lightly to dry it out and give it some crunch.

Remove the casing of the sausage and place the sausage meat in a small bowl. Add the cheese, salt and vinegar and, with a fork, blend the mixture together to form a paste.

Spread the sausage onto one side of each bread slice, right to the edges (so the crust doesn't burn), and place under a hot grill (broiler) until golden brown on top and cooked through.

MAKES 4 CROSTONI

Panini Tartufati

TRUFFLED SANDWICHES

50 g (1¾ oz) mascarpone

1 tablespoon finely grated parmesan cheese

1 teaspoon finely grated black truffle

4 mini brioche or soft finger buns, sliced in half lengthways

There is a not-so-secret spot for the most fabulous truffled sandwiches in Florence. Procacci, on via Tornabuoni, has been around since 1885 and has long been the place for one of these little truffled sandwiches and a glass of prosecco (or tomato juice – they're famous for this unusual combination). Although this isn't their special recipe, this one is easy to replicate at home and makes a dainty, special occasion sandwich when you can get your hands on fresh black truffles. Remember that a little goes a long way with these flavours.

Combine the mascarpone, parmesan and truffle in a mixing bowl until you have a creamy paste. Season with a pinch of salt. Spread 1 teaspoon of spread onto each little bun.

MAKES 4 SMALL BUNS

Panino *con* Finocchiona, Melanzane *e* Stracchino

PANINO WITH MARINATED EGGPLANT, FINOCCHIONA & STRACCHINO CHEESE

GRILLED EGGPLANT

1 medium eggplant (aubergine), sliced 5 mm (¼ in) thick

salt

1 small red bird's eye chilli, finely sliced

1 garlic clove, finely sliced

1 dried bay leaf

extra-virgin olive oil to cover

FOR EACH PANINO

1 square of Schiacciata (page 64) or focaccia

80 g (2¾ oz) stracchino cheese (or other good melting cheese)

40 g (1½ oz) finocchiona, sliced (see note)

2–3 slices grilled eggplant (aubergine)

NOTE

If you can't get finocchiona, you can substitute it with mortadella or some other salume – freshly sliced prosciutto is also very good. Stracchino cheese can be difficult to find outside Italy, but fresh mozzarella also makes a good substitute here.

This combination is inspired by my panino of choice at All'Antico Vinaio, a popular wine and panino bar in the shadow of the Palazzo Vecchio that attracts all types looking for a freshly made, cheap lunch. It's a mostly standing-room-only affair with patrons inevitably spilling out into the street, panino in hand, and a long queue at the height of lunch hour.

Finocchiona is a typical Tuscan cured meat – a large, round, pink salume often embedded with whole black peppercorns and that very Tuscan flavouring of wild fennel seeds. Soft and gooey stracchino cheese is ideal here, as it is creamy and delicately flavoured and does not overpower the other ingredients.

Generously salt the eggplant slices to help draw out their moisture. Leave for at least 30 minutes. Rinse thoroughly with cold water, drain and carefully pat them dry.

Cook the eggplant on a grill pan over medium heat. Cook until both sides are tender and browned. Place in a container with the chilli, garlic and bay leaf and cover with olive oil. This keeps well in the fridge for up to 1 week.

To prepare the panino, slice open the schiacciata or focaccia. Spread the stracchino on one side, layer with a few slices of finocchiona and 2–3 slices of eggplant. Serve as is or, if you prefer, warm it under a grill (broiler) or a sandwich press before serving.

SERVES 1

Panino *con* Spinaci *e* Brie

WARM BRIE & SPINACH ROLL

1 large bread roll, sliced in half
80 g (2¾ oz/⅓ cup) cooked, drained
  and chopped English spinach
  (about 1 bunch fresh, see page 117)
1 tablespoon extra-virgin olive oil
50 g (1¾ oz) brie, sliced

I used to pop by a tiny osteria, I Buongustai, on a narrow, medieval street in the centre of Florence and order this cheap and cheerful panino when on a tight break from work or study. You order by poking your head right into the windowed kitchen. It is often too busy to be able to sit down at a table, but you can perch on a bar stool in a corridor in front of the kitchen and watch the speedy Laura and Lucia in the kitchen and the hustle and bustle of customers coming in and out for lunch. This is a generous serve for one with a large roll, but you could make two smaller rolls with this filling if you prefer.

Warm the roll in the oven or under a grill (broiler) briefly.

Place the cooked spinach on one side of the roll, season with salt and pepper and drizzle over the olive oil. Top with slices of brie and place under the grill with the roll open. Grill until the cheese melts.

Close the panino and serve immediately.

SERVES 1

Panino *con* Lampredotto e Salsa Verde

LAMPREDOTTO PANINO WITH SALSA VERDE

8 crusty bread rolls

LAMPREDOTTO

1 celery stalk, roughly chopped
1 brown onion, roughly chopped
1 carrot, roughly chopped
1 tomato, roughly chopped
1 tablespoon salt
5 whole black peppercorns
1 kg (2 lb 3 oz) lampredotto
  (abomasum tripe)

SALSA VERDE

2 anchovy fillets
¼ onion, roughly chopped
½ garlic clove
1 bunch (about 100 g/3½ oz)
  flat-leaf parsley
10 basil leaves
2 heaped tablespoons salted capers,
  about 30–40 g (1–1½ oz), rinsed
juice of 1 lemon
60 ml (2 fl oz/¼ cup) extra-virgin
  olive oil

NOTE

You don't often find lampredotto
in small portions as it is generally
cooked and sold as a whole piece,
so if you have leftovers, you can
either freeze it for the next round
of panini or think about some creative
use – one of my favourite restaurants
in Florence, Il Magazzino, makes a
ravioli filling and meatballs with it,
two of the tastiest dishes in the city.

This is, without hesitation, the most Florentine dish of all. It is a tradition only found in the city of Florence, a sort of Renaissance fast food and still a favourite of the city's street food scene.

In Florence, the *lampredottai* (lampredotto vendors) not only make and sell panini filled with *lampredotto* (cooked abomasum tripe) but they will also sell you *lampredotto* already cooked in stock to take home, ready to be heated up and eaten as you like. Other than this panino, *lampredotto* is commonly used for meatballs (like the tripe meatballs on page 178) or in risotto. If you buy it directly from a butcher, most likely it has already been blanched, but you will still need to prepare it as described below.

Part of the joy of eating street food is watching the performance of it being prepared right in front of you. Here, the rolls are split open, perhaps with a bit of the bread in the middle removed to make room for the filling. The *lampredottaio* will take out a huge piece of *lampredotto* from a steaming, simmering pot, then roughly slice and chop it before generously heaping it onto a bread roll. It is seasoned with salt and pepper and topped with plenty of salsa verde (sometimes chilli, too). The final touch: with a fork pierced in the top half of the bread roll, it is dipped in the hot cooking broth to keep the panino juicy.

LAMPREDOTTO

Prepare a stock by adding all of the vegetable chunks and the tomato to 3 litres (101 fl oz/12 cups) water in a large pot with the salt and peppercorns. Bring to the boil and allow to simmer for about 30 minutes. Add the lampredotto, whole, and cook until soft, covered with a lid, for about 1 hour. Make sure the lampredotto is always submerged under the broth – add more water as necessary. Keep the lampredotto warm, in the broth, until you are ready to use it.

SALSA VERDE

Blend the anchovies, onion, garlic, herbs, capers and lemon juice together thoroughly in a food processor or with a stick blender, and add enough olive oil until you have a smooth, paste-like consistency. Season with salt and pepper.

PANINI

Roughly slice the lampredotto into 2 cm (¾ in) pieces. Slice the bread rolls in half and scoop out some of the bread from the middle to make room for the filling. Add some of the lampredotto to the bottom bread roll half, top with a heaping spoonful of salsa verde, season with salt and pepper, and dip the top of the bun into the cooking broth. Eat immediately.

MAKES ABOUT 8 HEARTY PANINI

Panino *con* Peposo

PANINO BOWL WITH BEEF STEW

1 large round, crusty roll
some warm beef stew such as Peposo
(page 204)

This is a clever way of converting leftover stew like *peposo* (page 204) into tomorrow's lunch. It's more an idea rather than a recipe and it is inspired by several of Florence's favourite panino shops, such as Semel, which borders the Sant'Ambrogio market or Il Cernacchino in the centre of town, a few steps away from Piazza Signoria. Use a large roll that has a good, thick, crunchy crust, as it will likely hold its shape better and withstand a bit of liquid.

Preheat the oven to 160°C (320°F).

Heat the roll in the oven until warm and the crust is crisp.

Slice the roll about two-thirds of the way up so the top of the roll is like a little lid. Pull out some of the inside of the roll to make room for the stew, leaving about 2 cm (¾ in) of bread all around the 'bowl'. Spoon the stew inside and top with the 'lid'. Eat with a fork. The stew's juices will slowly soak its way through the bread, creating an edible bowl which you can eat after you've finished the stew.

SERVES 1

Panino *con* Insalata Belga, Pecorino e Miele

PANINO WITH WITLOF, PECORINO AND HONEY

FOR EACH PANINO

2 slices of crusty Italian bread

2–3 slices young or semi-aged
   pecorino

1 teaspoon wildflower honey

4–5 witlof (Belgian endive/chicory)
   leaves, rinsed and patted dry

1 tablespoon extra-virgin olive oil

a pinch of salt

NOTE

If you can't get a suitable pecorino –
it should be rather soft to firm but not
too hard or crumbly – you could try
making this with provolone dolce or
asiago instead.

There is a hole-in-the-wall panino shop that looks over the Sant'Ambrogio market. It is so inconspicuous that you may walk past it several times before you even realise it's there. But keep an eye out for the hanging shelves, designed for holding little wine glasses while you eat your panino, standing. It's called Semel – named after the Florentine word for a type of bread roll – and has a small but unique menu of panini that changes with the seasons. One day perhaps there's donkey stew, on another there's anchovies with orange and fennel – it is definitely the place for more adventurous eaters and those who want to try something different, but the vegetarian offers will satisfy anyone.

This recipe is inspired by one such panino at Semel, which might be done with *valeriana*, a lovely, delicate salad leaf. Witlof (Belgian endive/chicory), with its slightly bitter, crunchy leaf, does a very nice job at balancing the sweetness of the honey and the salty bite of the pecorino cheese.

Lightly toast or warm the slices of bread.

Place the slices of pecorino on one slice of bread. Drizzle the honey over and arrange the witlof leaves on top. Dress with olive oil and salt. Top with the other slice of warm bread.

SERVES 1

Buontalenti's Gelato

According to popular legend, the first modern gelato was invented by a Florentine, the multi-talented artist, architect and engineer, Bernardo Buontalenti (1531–1608). This Mannerist artist and favourite architect of the Medici family was one of the key figures in Florence during Michelangelo's time. Among his works are the Forte Belvedere in Florence and the palace of Bianca Cappello; he helped complete the Uffizi and decorate the Boboli Gardens, and he fortified the city of Livorno. He was also a talented goldsmith and ceramicist, not to mention theatre set producer and event coordinator for the Medici dukes.

As the story goes, Buontalenti created a unique frozen dessert to present at a Medici banquet, designing a gelato machine where a closed cylinder containing a mixture of lemon, sugar, egg white and milk spun around a mixture of snow and salt to freeze the mixture. It was a sort of lemon sorbet to be served at the end of the meal in glasses. Today, there are a number of Florentine gelaterie that have created flavours such as *crema di buontalenti* or *crema fiorentina* that give a nod of credit to the Mannerist master.

Gelato *di* Riso

RICE GELATO

80 g (2¾ oz) risotto rice such
   as arborio or carnaroli
500 ml (17 fl oz/2 cups) full-cream
   (whole) cold milk
½ vanilla pod, seeds scraped
a pinch of salt
2 egg yolks
100 g (3½ oz) sugar
200 ml (7 fl oz) milk, warmed
zest of 1 orange
125 ml (4 fl oz/½ cup) well-chilled
   pouring (single/light) cream

NOTE

If making the gelato without an ice
cream machine, it is recommended
to serve on the day it is made, as it
will be creamier. If you want to make
it ahead of time and still have that
creamy gelato texture, an ice cream
machine is highly recommended.

There is a well-known Florentine gelateria that is particularly famous for its rice gelato but it's a flavour that you will find in all good artisan gelaterie. It's basically a rice pudding, whipped and frozen, so you have smooth, silky gelato with delightful little frozen pieces of rice.

Soak the rice for 30 minutes in cold water and drain. Place the rice in a saucepan with the cold milk, vanilla seeds and salt and cook over a low heat until the rice is very, very soft and the mixture becomes creamy. This should take about 30 minutes. Keep an eye on it, stir occasionally and be careful the bottom does not burn. Transfer the rice to a bowl and let it cool.

Prepare a crema (a pouring custard) by whisking the egg yolks with the sugar in a heatproof bowl until very pale and creamy. Add the warm milk, bit by bit, stirring with a wooden spoon until combined. Place the bowl over a bain marie or double boiler and cook gently over a medium heat, stirring continuously for 10 minutes, or until the eggs reach and stay at 70°C (160°F) for a few minutes. If you don't have a sugar thermometer to check the temperature, it should take about 10 minutes in total and the mixture should thicken ever so slightly and be hot, but not boiling. Draw your finger across the back of the spoon – the line should keep its shape for a few moments. Remove from the heat and stir the rice through the crema along with the orange zest. Chill the mixture thoroughly in the refrigerator.

Whip the chilled cream until soft peaks form and gently fold through the chilled rice mixture until combined. Chill in the refrigerator for 30 minutes, then place in an ice cream machine and churn according to manufacturer's instructions until frozen and creamy. Serve immediately for a softer style gelato or place the mixture in an airtight container in the freezer for at least 45 minutes to serve in scoops.

If you have stored the gelato in the freezer overnight or longer, let it stand for 15–20 minutes at room temperature to soften slightly before serving.

To make this without an ice cream machine, place the mixture in a sturdy, airtight 1 litre (34 fl oz) container with a fitted lid and freeze for about 5 hours. After around 4 hours, fluff the gelato with a fork. As it loosens, you can begin to beat it with the fork or spoon until the mixture is smooth and rather creamy. Return to the freezer for another hour or so. Fluff again to obtain a creamy and consistent texture before serving. If necessary, let it stand for 15–30 minutes to soften slightly before 'fluffing', beating to soften and serving in soft scoops.

MAKES ABOUT 1 LITRE (34 FL OZ/4 CUPS) OF GELATO (6-8 SERVES)

Gelato *al* Fior *di* Latte

MILK GELATO

500 ml (17 fl oz/2 cups) full-cream
   (whole) milk
150 g (5½ oz) sugar
250 ml (8½ fl oz/1 cup) pouring
   cream (single/light), chilled

NOTE

It is best to make this creamy gelato
with an ice cream machine.

Homemade gelato usually benefits
from a rest in the freezer for about
an hour before serving if you have
just made it. Or if it's been in the
freezer overnight or even longer,
take it out of the freezer about
15 minutes before serving.

Gelato is a true Florentine tradition that can be traced back to the
Renaissance. As one story goes, the secret recipe for this frozen dessert
passed from a modest Florentine poultry vendor to the courts of Catherine
de' Medici during a competition to find the most unique dish that had
ever been seen. The frozen dessert of 'sugared and perfumed' ice was
considered so remarkable that Catherine de' Medici brought the recipe to
Paris to impress the French court.

Made from just three ingredients, this particular gelato is as wholesome
and simple as can be. Perhaps that's what makes it a popular flavour with
children and adults alike. Marco is known for only ever ordering *fior di
latte* at any gelateria he ever goes to, never wavering once in his decision
in all the years I've known him – today our daughter will ask at a gelateria
for '*preferito di babbo*' (Dad's favourite) when she wants this flavour,
which is her own favourite too.

Combine the milk and sugar together in a saucepan over a low–medium heat. It
should not boil, but just reach the point where tiny bubbles appear around the
edges of the pan. Take the pan off the heat.

Cover and allow to cool to room temperature. Add the cream and churn in an
ice cream machine according to the manufacturer's instructions until frozen and
creamy but firm.

Serve immediately for a softer style gelato or place the mixture in an airtight
container in the freezer for at least 45 minutes to serve in scoops.

MAKES ABOUT 900 ML (30 FL OZ) OF GELATO (6-8 SERVES)

Sorbetto *di* Susine

PLUM SORBET

500 g (1 lb) whole, ripe dark plums,
   such as damson or blood plums
100 g (3½ oz) sugar
juice of ½ large lemon

NOTE

While this is achievable without
an ice cream machine, the results
will be somewhat less creamy on
the palate.

In the summer, when stone fruit is abundant, mountains of plums, peaches, nectarines and apricots fill the markets and you can buy them by the bucketload for next to nothing. It's an age old tradition to make jam from the overflow of too much ripe fruit, especially if you happen to have fruit trees (every summer my brother-in-law's mother, Ariana, is busy making enough plum jam to keep the pantry stocked for a year), but *sorbetto* or sorbet is another wonderful way to preserve ripe, seasonal fruit. I have always loved Artusi's recipes for gelato and although he does not have one for plums, he does have simple recipes for other stone fruit *sorbetti*, such as apricot or buttery white Florentine peaches known as *pesche burrone*, an heirloom variety that's hard to find today. But it's the bright colour of damson or blood plums that I really love about this *sorbetto*, and the beauty of this recipe is that is it so low maintenance – throw the plums in the pot, skins, pits and all. Strain them later.

Rinse the plums and, without drying them, place them whole in a saucepan over low–medium heat with 60 ml (2 fl oz/¼ cup) water, covered, and bring to a simmer. As they heat, the plums will release their own juices. Check regularly and stir occasionally to make sure they do not stick to the bottom and burn. As they get soft, break them up a little with your wooden spoon. Once simmering, uncover, lower the heat and cook until the plums have released all their juices and have essentially 'melted' down, softening completely, about 10–15 minutes, depending on their size. Remove from the heat and strain the mixture over a bowl (discard the pits) with a food mill or simply with the use of a spatula and a fine-meshed strainer. Set aside to cool.

Place the sugar in a small saucepan with 125 ml (4 fl oz/½ cup) water. Bring to the boil to dissolve the sugar. As soon as it begins to boil, remove from the heat. Let cool slightly then add to the strained plums along with the lemon juice. Let the mixture chill completely before churning in an ice cream machine according to the manufacturer's instructions. Serve immediately for a soft sorbet or place the mixture in an airtight container in the freezer for about an hour longer to serve in scoops.

Without an ice cream machine, pour the mixture into a sturdy, shallow container with an airtight lid and place in the freezer for about 5 hours. When frozen, use a fork or spoon to loosen and 'fluff' the sorbet. As it loosens, you can begin to beat it with the fork or spoon until the mixture is smooth and rather creamy. Place back in the freezer and freeze for a further hour. If frozen overnight or longer, it will have hardened and will need to be left at room temperature for about 15–20 minutes to soften slightly before 'fluffing', then beating to soften and serving in soft scoops.

MAKES ABOUT 500 ML (17 FL OZ/2 CUPS) (ABOUT 4 SERVES)

Address Book

A note on Florentine addresses: you may find, confusingly, that a street has two doors with the same numbers, or that when looking for an address that numbers don't apparently go in order down the street. Take a closer look at the colour of the street number – it will either be black/blue or red. Black or dark blue is for residences while red is for businesses. Written business addresses also have an "R" (for *rosso*, or red) immediately following the number.

Pasticcerie *e* bar
PASTRY SHOPS AND CAFES

Places to go for an Italian-style breakfast (coffee and a pastry) in the morning or an aperitivo in the evening. The *bar* is also a refuge at any time of the day for a refuel – whether it's for coffee, ice-cold water or a sweet or savoury snack chosen from the glass counter. Standing at the bar is the local preference – expect to pay a little more when you sit down.

RIVOIRE
Piazza della Signoria 5. Convenient for its proximity to the Palazzo Vecchio and the Uffizi, this classic Florentine *bar* is pricey so avoid sitting down. Take away or stand at the counter for a coffee and a pastry before heading out to see Botticelli.

CAFFÈ GIACOSA
via della Spada 10r. Roberto Cavalli's stylish cafe also serves excellent coffee and small pastries, savoury and sweet. A good place for a negroni, too: it was invented in this very spot in 1919.

PROCACCI
via de' Tornabuoni 64r. An historic *bar* with a fashionable address, come here for a snack of dainty truffle panini and a prosecco or tomato juice.

PASTICCERIA GIORGIO
via Duccio di Boninsegna 36. Although outside the historical centre, it's worth a hop on the tram to get to this elegant pastry shop for one of their spectacular crema-filled pastries. Their *schiacciata alla fiorentina* is a favourite and they also do a fantastic aperitivo.

Forni
BAKERIES

The bakery is a busy place in the morning and at lunchtime, when people flock to buy bread, sweet baked goods or ready-to-eat snacks such as *schiacciata*, *schiacciatine* and pizza by the slice.

FOCACCERIA PUGI
Piazza San Marco 9b. Look for the ticket holder and grab a number – this place gets busy when it's snack time! Their focaccia, *schiacciata* and pizze are very popular.

S. FORNO
via Santa Monaca 3. A chic bakery run by the same people as Il Santino and Il Santo Bevitore (see overleaf).

CANTINETTA DEI VERAZZANO
via dei Tavolini 18r. The main entrance to the little restaurant of this historical winemaking legacy is a wonderful bakery with excellent *schiacciatine* topped with seasonal vegetables, and biscotti, in particular. They are also one of the few places that always have *cecina* or *torta di ceci*, a besan (chickpea flour) crepe-like specialty.

Mercati
MARKETS AND FOOD SHOPPING

If shopping for food to take home and cook, my preference is the Sant'Ambrogio market – it's authentic and un-touristy, so much more practical for food shopping. If you're in the Oltrarno and don't fancy going all the way to Sant'Ambrogio, Piazza Santo Spirito has a small, charming, outdoor market (a handful of fruit and vegetable stalls, plus household goods, clothing, shoes etc) every morning.

MERCATO CENTRALE

via del Ariento. Open all day, every day, the upstairs section of this covered market is a modern, stylish – and pumping – food court. Downstairs you can still find some of the traditional food vendors – Nerbone still serves classic, no-frills Florentine fare.

MERCATO SANT'AMBROGIO

Piazza Lorenzo Ghiberti. A covered market like the Central Market, here you will find the fruit and vegetable stands outside, while indoors are meat, poultry and fish vendors, an excellent fresh pasta shop, bakeries, dry goods and an extremely cheap and cheerful trattoria.

MERCATO SANTO SPIRITO

Piazza Santo Spirito. An outdoor market with a handful of stalls and a local, colourful feel to it.

BIZZARI

via della Condotta 32r. An historical, apothecary-like shop where you buy things out of jars. The artisan candied fruit, spices and unusual ingredients are a good excuse to come in here.

FATTORIA SAN MICHELE

via dei Rustici 6r. A hole-in-the-wall shop front down an alley not far from Palazzo Vecchio that sells excellent organic olive oil and wine grown on their estate just 15 km (about 9 miles) outside of Florence, as well as fresh pasta made to order.

ANZUINI E MASSI MACCELLERIA

via de' Neri 84r. An historic butcher dating to the end of the 1800s. Worth a stop for their housemade salumi, in particular the *finocchiona*.

Trattorie
TRATTORIAS

There are many restaurants to choose from in central Florence but these are my pick of the ones that offer classic, traditional Florentine fare at average prices.

ALLA VECCHIA BETTOLA

via Luigi Ariosto 34r. On the edge of Florence's Piazza Tasso in the San Frediano neighbourhood, this classic osteria is the big brother of Nerbone in the Central Market.

BRINDELLONE

Piazza Piattellina 10/11r. An off-the-beaten-path restaurant near Piazza del Carmine and a good choice for *bistecca*.

OSTERIA DEL CAFFÈ ITALIANO

via Isola delle Stinche 11/13r. In addition to the classic Florentine fare, they have an excellent pizzeria next door, too.

TRATTORIA LA CASALINGA

via dei Michelozzi 9r. This institute in the Santo Spirito quarter is a favourite local family restaurant.

TRATTORIA DA BURDE

via Pistoiese 6r. Outside the historic centre but worth a trip for those looking for a seasonal and traditional local restaurant serving things up just as the Florentines love.

DA RUGGERO

via Senese 89r. A jewel of a trattoria just a little outside of the Porta Romana gateway.

I BUONGUSTAI

via de' Cerchi 15r. Down a side street off Piazza della Signoria, this tiny but reliable lunchtime space fills up very quickly. You can also simply grab a panino and sit in the corridor watching the amazing ladies in the kitchen cook up a storm.

OSTERIA TRIPPERIA IL MAGAZZINO

Piazza della Passera 2–3r. Set in the most charming piazza in Florence, this place specialises in – and does magic with – offal, but not exclusively. One of my favourites.

RISTORANTE DEL FAGIOLI

Corso de' Tintori 47r. Always reliable, always a favourite.

SABATINO

via Pisana 2r. A very cheap, no-frills family restaurant in the San Frediano quarter.

TRATTORIA SOSTANZA TROIA

via del Porcellana 25r. A classy and historic trattoria – come here for the butter chicken and the *bistecca*. Cash only.

TRATTORIA MARIO

via della Rosina 2r. San Lorenzo quarter, near the Mercato Centrale.

Paninoteche
PANINI SPOTS

From food vans to hole-in-the-walls, Florence has an excellent selection of places for a quick, cheap, made-on-the-spot panino and a little glass of wine.

I DUE FRATELLINI
via de' Cimatori 38r. In a side street near Piazza della Signoria.

CASA DEL VINO
via dell'Ariento 16r. Hidden near the San Lorenzo markets, it's easy to miss this charming and historic wine bar and panino spot.

ALL ANTICO VINAIO
via de' Neri 65r. Just behind Palazzo Vecchio, this popular sandwich spot gets busy so get here early or come in the early evening for an aperitivo-like snack, standing on the street.

SERGIO POLLINI TRIPPAIO
corner of via de' Macci and Borgo la Croce (near the Sant'Ambrogio market). This food van run by a father and son team is famous for its *lampredotto* panini.

SEMEL
Piazza Ghiberti 44r. Next to the Sant'Ambrogio markets, this creative panino place is so tiny, blink and you'll miss it – but try not to, it's really wonderful.

Enoteche
WINE BARS

There are only a few proper wine bars in Florence but they are good ones and all worth a visit for a glass of wine. Or more.

VOLPI E L'UVA
Piazza dei Rossi 1. A great wine bar next to the Santa Felicità church – pop in and put in a coin to turn the lights on to see Pontormo's fresco of the Deposition on your way there.

PITTI GOLA E CANTINA
Piazza Pitti 16. Wine and dine with a view of Pitti Palace.

IL SANTINO
via di Santo Spirito 60r. An atmospheric wine bar in a historic palazzo – also a good spot to wait for a table at next door's Il Santo Bevitore.

Gelaterie
GELATO

Gelato abounds in Florence, but there's gelato (the sort displayed in hideous, giant, brightly coloured mountains) and then there's real, properly made, artisan gelato (soft and smooth, subtly coloured with natural ingredients and stored in deep tubs, sometimes hidden completely out of sight). It's worthwhile seeking out the latter and these are a few of my favourites.

CARABÈ
via Ricasoli 60r. Sicilian-style gelato and granita near the Accademia Gallery.

VESTRI
Borgo degli Albizi 11r. An artisan chocolate shop that also makes wonderful gelato, hidden away in metal tubs under the counter.

PERCHÈ NO
via Tavolini 19r. A busy gelateria in the centre of town with interesting flavours such as sesame or rose.

GELATERIA DEI NERI
via dei Neri 9r. A wide selection of flavours at this popular gelateria in the shadow of Palazzo Vecchio.

GELATERIA DELLA PASSERA
via Toscanella, 15r. A tiny, pretty gelateria in an equally pretty piazza with a small selection of unique flavours.

Glossary

ALCHERMES

Also spelled Alkermes, this Tuscan liqueur dates to the Middle Ages. Stained bright pink by cochineal insects and perfumed with spices such as cinnamon, vanilla and cloves, it was once used as a restorative, pick-me-up tonic. Today, it's a vital ingredient in Tuscan desserts such as *zuccotto*, but it is rarely consumed on its own.

ARTUSI

Pellegrino Artusi is commonly thought of as the great-grandfather of Italian cuisine, thanks to his cookbook, *Science in the Kitchen and the Art of Eating Well,* filled with 790 recipes and self-published in 1891. It made its way into households all over the recently unified Italy. Although from Emilia-Romagna, Artusi lived in Florence for many years (and wrote the cookbook while there), so many of his recipes are Tuscan, and even more specifically, Florentine, making him a constant reference for Florentine cuisine today.

CANTUCCINI

Tuscan 'biscotti' are usually filled with nuts but sometimes chocolate or dried fruit and baked twice for extra crunch, so they can withstand being dunked in vin santo – a traditional way to finish a meal.

CICCIA

In Tuscan slang, this word means 'meat' but it is also used as an affectionate term for a female friend or relative (*ciccio* for masculine).

FINOCCHIONA

A large, round, very fine and soft, pink salame flavoured with wild fennel seeds, which is also what gives it its name (*finocchio* means 'fennel'). According to legend, it was invented after a thief stole a stick of salame at a fair near Prato and hid it in a field of wild fennel. When he went to collect it a few days later, he found the salame had absorbed the wonderful scent of the fennel. Genius.

FLOUR

Plain flour is known by the numbers '00' and '0' in Italian, which refers to the size of the grains after milling. Both are soft flours and, because of their generally low gluten content and soft texture, are best for baking cakes and light breads. Hard or 'strong' flour, such as durum flour (*semolino* in Italian), is used for making fresh pasta and strong bread, as the high gluten content makes the dough elastic and holds its shape well during cooking.

LAMPREDOTTO

The fourth stomach of a cow (known as abomasum in English), this is rarely found in any other cuisine but it is a typically Florentine preparation to boil it in stock and serve it sliced in a soft bun with salsa verde (a green sauce with a parsley base) and perhaps a hint of chilli. The top of the bun is usually dipped in the hot broth before serving. This is usually eaten directly at a food van, where it is prepared by the *lampredottaio* on the spot.

LARDO

Not lard (which is *strutto* in Italian), as many mistakenly think, but cured pork back fat. Although there is really no substitute for this silky, melt-in-the-mouth, flavour-packed product, you could use prosciutto crudo or pancetta in its place, depending on the recipe.

PECORINO

A Tuscan sheep's milk cheese that can take the place of Parmesan when it is *stagionato* (aged) for grating, or can be part of an antipasto or cheese platter served with honey when it is *semi-stagionato* (semi-aged or mild and young).

POPONE

The Tuscan word for *melone* (cantaloupe or rockmelon). You'll often find it paired with prosciutto as a summery antipasto.

RAMERINO

The Tuscan word for *rosmarino* (rosemary). You'll find it in *pandiramerino*, a sweet raisin and rosemary bun.

SANGIOVESE

The black grape that makes up the major part of Tuscany's favourite wines, such as Chianti, Brunello di Montalcino and Vino Nobile di Montepulciano – food-friendly wines that naturally go well with all traditional Tuscan food.

SCARPETTA

The act of mopping up the leftover sauce on your plate with a piece of bread, it comes from the word *scarpa* (shoe) and is one of the reasons restaurants always give you a basket of bread.

SCIOCCO

The Tuscan word for bland. Elsewhere in Italy this means 'silly' but there really is nothing silly at all about Tuscan bread, which is *sciocco*, as it is unsalted.

SOFFRITTO

The base of all good *sughi* (sauces) in Tuscan cooking. In general, this consists of finely chopped onion, carrot and celery, sauteed gently in olive oil.

TRUFFLES

Tartufi are a prized ingredient found best in autumn but there are also smaller, pungent summer and spring versions (*marzuolo* or 'March', for example). White truffles come from the town of San Miniato, between Florence and Pisa, and are some of the best in the world. When in season, you'll find *tartufi* used as freshly as possible (just grated over the top) over fried eggs or pasta.

VIN SANTO

Literally meaning 'Holy wine', this is Tuscany's famous amber-coloured dessert wine. Enjoy it at the end of a meal in a very small glass with *cantuccini* to dunk into it. It can also be used in cooking but without it, substitute with another sweet wine or marsala.

ZENZERO

An old-fashioned Tuscan word for *peperoncino* (chilli) – you might still find it in old cookbooks, for example. Confusingly, in Italian, *zenzero* means ginger. But don't be mistaken – there is no ginger in Tuscan cooking.

References

I thoroughly recommend these books for anyone wanting to delve more into Florentine (or Italian in general) cuisine and food history – many of these may only be available in Italian but if language is no barrier, they are worth a look and perhaps a cook out of too (Artusi's book is available in English and Ada Boni's is translated in an abridged version known simply as *The Talisman*). All of these are well used in my house.

A non-cookbook that I thoroughly recommend for more detailed information on every single little aspect of Florence's history is Eve Borsook's *The Companion Guide to Florence*. Published in 1997, it is still perfectly valid and is an excellent way to learn about Florence and the lifestyles of Florentines throughout history. It's heavy, but worth taking around Florence with you as your guide.

Artusi, Pellegrino 1960, *Scienza in Cucina e l'Arte di Mangiare Bene*, Giunti Marzocco, Firenze.

Boni, Ada 1999, *Il Talismano della Felicità*, Editore Colombo, Roma.

Camporesi, Carla Geri 2007, *Ricette Tradizionali Fiorentine*, Maria Pacini Fazzi Editore, Lucca.

David, Elizabeth 2011, *Italian Food*, revised edition, Penguin, London.

Field, Carol 1985, *The Italian Baker*, reissue edition, Harper & Rowe, New York.

Petroni, Paolo 2009, *La vera Cucina Toscana*, Giunti Editore, Firenze.

Riley, Gillian 2007, *The Oxford Companion to Italian Food*, Oxford University Press, New York.

Romanelli Leonardo, Carlo Macchi and Nanni Ricci 1997, *Ricette di Osteria di Firenze e Chianti: Desinari di casa tra città e contado*, Slow Food Editore, Bra.

Santini, Aldo 1992, *Cucina Fiorentina*, Franco Muzzio Editore, Padova.

Salemi, Maria 2010, *Città del Gusto: Firenze, Souvenir gastronomico tra Arte, Cultura e Tradizione*, Nardini Editore, Firenze.

About the Author

I grew up in an international household – a Japanese mother and an Australian father, living in Beijing, China. So it was inevitable that I found myself halfway around the world later in life – first moving to the US for a degree in Fine Art from Rhode Island School of Design, and then Italy, which strangely felt like a place I finally could belong to.

I made my first move to Florence on a whim when I was twenty, arriving at Santa Maria Novella station with nothing but a suitcase and some broken Italian. I spent a semester studying etching in a converted horse stable and living within earshot of the bells of the Basilica of Santa Croce with an apartment full of international students. I loved it.

I was immediately drawn in by the charms of the Renaissance city, how every stone, every corner is steeped in history and how the food, stubbornly but comfortingly unchanging, tells a story and brings people together. I have always loved cooking and always loved food, and found it's the best way to understand a place and its culture.

I moved back again to Florence four years later, this time to study darkroom photography and art restoration. I followed in the footsteps of many expatriates before me, who visit Florence and fall hopelessly in love with it (or someone from it). In my case it was both.

The first time I ever cooked for Marco (a humble, impromptu plate of pasta made in my tiny studio apartment with my two-burner stove top – one of which was broken – with what I happened to have in my minibar of a fridge), he must have been impressed as he said, 'I'll marry you.' And he did, a few years later, inside the Palazzo Vecchio. Florence was our home for five years together before we moved to Australia, where our daughter was born, for a three year stint. But Italy kept calling us back and we now call Tuscany home again.

I continue writing the blog that I began while living in Florence – it is dedicated to telling the stories behind regional and historical Italian dishes, particularly Tuscan, in the context of my family life, which involves a quickly growing toddler, our travels or our everlasting debate over whether we belong in Australia or Italy. I also write a weekly recipe column, 'Regional Italian Food', on regional recipes for New York-based website *Food52* and a bi-monthly column '*I Classici a Pranzo*' in Italian for the food website of Italy's leading newspaper, *Corriere della Sera*.

Acknowledgements

There are two people who inspired me enormously while writing this book. One is Pellegrino Artusi, who although not even Tuscan, lived in Florence for many years and wrote often about the city, its people and included many of their recipes in his cookbook in 1891.

The other is my husband, Marco Lami. When we first met, Marco had never actually ever cooked a single thing, but anyone who knows him now, knows that he is an exceptional and always curious cook. The kitchen is the life and heart of our home and it's where we gather or cook together every day. Many of the dishes in this book are ones we cook at home regularly, and in fact, some of these recipes are Marco's own, like the *sugo toscano* and his beloved *fegatelli*. Without him and his constant support this book would not be what it is.

Thank you to the entire Hardie Grant dream team in Melbourne: Paul, Jane, Hannah, Mark, Lucy and Susie, as well as Allison Colpoys who made the pages of this book come alive. I am still in awe of the experience and talent I watched unfold before my very eyes for the recipe shots: Caroline Jones and Jemima Good, who were with me in the kitchen, Deb Kaloper styling our dishes and Lauren Bamford shooting. I could not have dreamed up a better result. I would also like to thank Kate Pollard, publisher from Hardie Grant UK's office in London, who first contacted me with the idea of making a cookbook and set the wheels in motion for making a dream come true.

I am ever grateful to my parents, my husband and my daughter (who was only 18 months old when it all began!) for their never-ending patience, support and much taste-testing and dish washing over the past year or so. A very special thank you goes to my sister, Hana, who came all the way to Florence with me, lent me her camera and carried bags and entertained a toddler, while inspiring many of the location shots. Hana is also credited for taking the beautiful photo of me and my daughter on the last page of this book. Grazie to my mother-in-law, Angela, especially for recounting family food stories to me.

A heartfelt thanks to my friends and fellow food writers who have provided support and inspiration during the cookbook writing process, in particular Emma Galloway, Rachel Roddy, Kirsteen Travers, Giulia Scarpaleggia and Regula Yswijn.

Finally, I am eternally grateful to the wonderful friends and strangers from every corner of the world who enthusiastically volunteered to test and taste my recipes at home. Their notes, comments and suggestions have helped fine tune many of the recipes and have ultimately made the book what it is today. Thank you!

Giulia Barbini, Jill Bernardini, Becky Bishop, Nathalie Boisard-Beudin, Natasha Boom, Peter, Jane and Tobias Brown, Nat Burke, Julia Busuttil, Valerie Caron, Sophie Chamberlin, Garima Chugh, Annabelle Cooke, Sabrina Corti, Lexi Earl, Oriana El-Khoury, Ilaria Falorsi, Jasmina Gajic, Sara Getz, Michelle Graham, Sasha Gora, Em Hart, Carly Haase, Caroline Hamilton, Stephanie Henricks, Julie Mia Holmes, Michelle Jung, Cait Kirkpatrick, Heilala von Keyserlingk, Kate Knapp, Robyn Laing, Shirley Lee, Shiru Lim, Liz Lindstrom, Michelle Louw, Sandra Lupton, Adelina Pereira Marghidan, Elena Makarov, Jill Malek, Max Brearley, Julia Mon Cureno, Kara & Andrew Muratore, Ingrid Oosterhuis, Audrey Osuna, Kit Palaskas, Amelia Pane Schaffner, Kevin Parker & Donna Pancari, Helga Pojani, Giulia Porro, Anna Pogson, Christine Pobke, Carmen Pricone, Erika Rax, Sophia Real, Sneh Roy, Carly Slater, Gabrielle Schafner, Nina Sparling, Julia Spiess, Barbara Sweeney, Janie Trayer, Veronica Fossa, Anja Vecchi, Niranjana Viswanathan, Cassady Walters, Jennifer Williams, Brenna Wilson, Michael Woodward, Rebecca Yorston, Jessica Zawicki, Gianna Zuch.

Also thank you to Andrei Davidoff, Market Import, Safari Living and Perfect Pieces who lent us beautiful pieces for the recipe shots.

Index

Published in 2016 by Hardie Grant Books

Hardie Grant Books (Australia)
Ground Floor, Building 1
658 Church Street
Richmond, Victoria 3121
www.hardiegrant.com.au

Hardie Grant Books (UK)
5th & 6th Floors
52–54 Southwark Street
London SE1 1UN
www.hardiegrant.co.uk

A Cataloguing-in-Publication entry is available from the catalogue
of the National Library of Australia at www.nla.gov.au

Florentine: The true cuisine of Florence
9781743790038

Publishing director: Jane Willson
Project editor: Hannah Koelmeyer
Editor: Susie Ashworth
Design manager: Mark Campbell
Cover design: Kasia Gadecki & Allison Colpoys
Internal design: Allison Colpoys
Marble patterns: Kasia Gadecki & Allison Colpoys
Food photography: Lauren Bamford
Location photography: Emiko Davies
Author photographs: Hana Davies
Stylist: Deb Kaloper
Home economists: Caroline Jones and Jemima Good
Production manager: Todd Rechner

Colour reproduction by Splitting Image Colour Studio
Printed and bound in China by 1010